Spell it yourself

ford University Press

Oxford University Press, Walton Street, Oxford OX2 6DP

Oxford   New York   Toronto
Delhi   Bombay   Calcutta   Madras   Karachi
Petaling   Jaya   Singapore   Hong Kong   Tokyo
Nairobi   Dar es Salaam   Cape Town
Melbourne   Auckland

and associated companies in
Berlin   Ibadan

Oxford is a trade mark of Oxford University Press

ISBN 0 19 834135 0 paperback

First edition 1962
Reprinted 1965, 1971, 1973,
1976, 1977, 1978, 1979
Second edition 1981
Reprinted 1983, 1984, 1986, 1987, 1988, 1989, 1990,
1991, 1992

ISBN 0 19 834138 5 hardback

First published 1992

Filmset by Tradespools Limited, Frome, Somerset
Printed in Great Britain at The Bath Press, Avon

Contents

Instructions

1   Think hard about the word you wish to spell and try to decide with which two letters it starts.

2   Find these two letters in the Index and you will see the number of the page where the word can be found or where you should begin looking for it.

3   Turn to this page and look down the column under these two letters until you find the word you want. Where there are a lot of words which begin with the same two letters, the first three letters of the words are given at the top of the column to help you find the word you want.

It may be necessary to add the word endings shown in *italics* on the right-hand side of the column in order to build up the complete word you want, e.g.

rich   *er, est, ly, ness, es*
hair   *dresser, -dryer, pin, -slide, -style, s*

Here the words **richer, richest, richly, richness** and **riches** may be built up, and also **hairdresser(s), hair-dryer(s), hairpins(s), hair-slide(s), hair-style(s)** and **hairs.**

Where the last letter or letters of a word are in *italics* these must be left off before adding to the other endings, e.g.

happ*y*   *ier, iest, ily, iness.*

Here the *y* must be left off before making:

happier, happiest, happily, happiness.

The plurals of most nouns may be formed by adding the letter, or letters, shown in *italics* on the extreme right of the column. A few nouns have their plurals given in full on the right of the column, and you will notice that some nouns have two plurals, either of which may be used, e.g. **cactuses** or **cacti, hoofs** or **hooves, fish** or **fishes.**

All the words with *ed, ing* after them are verbs or may be used as verbs. If you require the word to end in either *ed* or *ing*, remember the following:

(a) **kick** *ed, ing, s* = **kicked   kicking   kicks**

Here *ed* or *ing* or *s* may be added to the verb without changing the word at all.

(b) **stab** *bed, bing, s* = **stabbed   stabbing   stabs**
  stop *ped, ping, s* = **stopped   stopping   stops**

Here you can see that the final consonant (the last letter) of these verbs has to be doubled before adding *ed* or *ing*.

(c) **blame** *d, ℓing, s* = **blamed   blaming   blames**

Where a verb ends in a letter **e** the *d* or *s* may be added to the word but the **e** must be dropped before adding *ing*. An *ℓ* is placed before the *ing* to remind you of this.

There are a few other verbs which change their endings in different ways. You will usually find these endings printed by the side of, above or below, the verb, e.g.

began		**lie**	*d, s*	**carry**	*ing*
begin	*ning, s*	**lying**		**carr** *ied*	*ies*
begun					

Warning: A word which has a star (*) after it has the same sound, or almost the same sound, as another word; but it has a different meaning and spelling, e.g. **knew* new*; their* there*; which* witch*.** The word endings will help you to decide which of these words you want and so will the words in brackets. These are included to guide you; they are not always exact definitions. The words are paired in small print at the bottom of the page. If you find that you have looked up the wrong word you may easily see how the other is spelt and where it may be found in its correct alphabetical place in the book.

ab

ac

ab	
abandon	ed, ing, ment, s
abate	d, ℯing, ment, s
abbess	es
abbey	s
abbot	s
abduct	ed, ing, ion, s
abhor	red, ring, rence, rent, s
abide	d, ℯing, s
abilit y	ies
ablaze	
able	r, st, -bodied
abnormal	ity, ly
aboard	
abolish	ed, ing, es
abominable	
abominate	d, ℯing, s
Aboriginal	s or Aborigines
abound	ed, ing, s
about	
above	-board
abreast	
abroad	
abrupt	ly, ness
abscess	es
absence	s
absent	ed, ing, ly, ee, s
absent-minded	ly, ness
absolute	ly
absorb	ed, ing, ent, s
abstain	ed, ing, s
absurd	ity, ly
abundance	
abundant	ly
abuse	d, ℯing, s
abysmal	ly
abyss	es

ac	
academ y	ies
accelerate	d, ℯing, s
accent	s
accept* (receive)	able, ed, ing, s
accident	al, ally, s
accommodate	d, ℯing, s
accommodation	
accompany	ing
accompan ied	ies
accomplish	ed, ing, es
according	ly
account	ed, ing, ant, s
accumulate	d, ℯing, s
accuracy	
accurate	ly
accusation	s
accuse	d, ℯing, s
accustom	ed, ing, s
ache	d, ℯing, s
achieve	d, ℯing, ment, s
acid	s
acknowledge	d, ℯing, s
acknowledg(e)ment	s
acorn	s
acquaint	ed, ing, ance, s
acquire	d, ℯing, ment, s
acre	age, s
acrobat	ic, s
across	
act	ed, ing, s
actor	s
actress	es
action	s
active	ly
activit y	ies
actual	ly

ℯ Drop **e** before adding *ing*

* accept
except

ad   ae af ag

ad	
adapt	*able, ed, ing, or, s*
add	*ed, ing, s*
addition	*al, s*
adder	*s*
address	*ed, ing, es*
adequate	*ly*
adhere	*d, ℓing, s*
adhesive	*s*
adjective	*s*
adjoin	*ed, ing, s*
adjust	*able, ed, ing, ment, s*
admirabl*e*	*y*
admiral	*s*
admiration	
admire	*d, ℓing, r, s*
admission	*s*
admit	*ted, ting, s*
admittance	
adopt	*ed, ing, ion, s*
adorabl*e*	*y*
adore	*d, ℓing, s*
adorn	*ed, ing, ment, s*
adrift	
adult	*s*
advance	*d, ℓing, ment, s*
advantage	*s*
adventure	*d, ℓing, r, s*
adventurous	*ly, ness*
adverb	*s*
adversar*y*	*ies*
advertise	*d, ℓing, r, s*
advertisement	*s*
advice	
advisable	
advise	*d, ℓing, r, s*
advocate	*d, ℓing, s*

ae	
aerial	*s*
aerodrome	*s*
aeronaut	*ic, s*
aeroplane	*s*

af	
affair	*s*
affect	*ed, ing, s*
affection	*s*
affectionate	*ly, ness*
affix	*ed, ing, es*
afford	*ed, ing, s*
afloat	
afraid	
after	
afternoon	*s*
afterwards	

ag	
again	
against	
age	*d, less, -group, s*
ageing or aging	
agent	*s*
aggravate	*d, ℓing, s*
aggressive	*ly, ness*
aghast	
agile	*ly*
agilit*y*	*ies*
agitate	*d, ℓing, s*
ago	
agonize	*d, ℓing, s*
agon*y*	*ies*
agree	*able, d, ing, ment, s*
agricultur*e*	*al*
aground	

ℓ Drop **e** before adding *ing*

ai

aid	ed, ing, s
ail* (be ill)	ed, ing, ment, s
aim	ed, ing, less, lessly, s
air*	ed, ing, crew, mail, tight, man, men
air*	gun, field, line, port, way, s
aircraft	-carrier
Airedale	s
air force	s
air y	ier, iest, ily, iness
aisle* (part of a church; gangway)	s

al

alarm	ed, ing, ist, -bell, -clock, s
album	s
alcohol	ism, ic, s
alcove	s
ale* (beer)	s
alert	ed, ing, ly, ness, s
algebra	
alibi	s
alien	s
alight	ed, ing, s
alike	
alive	
all right	
alley	way, s
alligator	s
allot	ted, ting, ment, s
allow	*ed, ing, ance, s
all y	ies
almond	-blossom, -paste, -tree, s
almost	
alone	
along	side
aloud* (loudly)	

alphabet	ical, ically, s
already	
Alsatian	s
also	
altar* (church table)	s
alter* (change)	ed, ing, ation, s
alternate	d, ∉ing, ly, s
alternative	ly, s
although	
altitude	s
altogether	
aluminium	
always	

am

amateur	ish, s
amaze	d, ∉ing, ment, s
amber	
ambition	s
ambitious	ly, ness
amble	d, ∉ing, s
ambulance	man, men, s
ambush	ed, ing, es
amend	ed, ing, ment, s
amiabl e	y
amid or **amidst**	
amiss	
ammunition	
among or **amongst**	
amount	ed, ing, s
amphibian	s or **amphibia**
amphibious	ly
ample	r, st, ness
amplifier	s
amputate	d, ∉ing, s
amuse	d, ∉ing, ment, s

∉ Drop **e** before adding *ing*

*	ail	air	aisle	allowed	altar
	ale	heir	isle	aloud	alter

an   ap

an	
anaesthetic	s
ancestor	s
ancestr y	ies
anchor	ed, ing, age, s
ancient	ly, ness, s
anemone	s
angel	s
anger	ed, ing, s
angr y	ier, iest, ily
angle	d, ẹing, r, s
anguish	ed, ing, es
animal	s
ankle	s
anniversar y	ies
announce	d, ẹing, r, ment, s
annoy	ed, ing, ance, s
annual	ly, s
anoint	ed, ing, ment, s
anonymous	ly
anorak	s
another	
answer	ed, ing, s
ant	-eater, -hill, s
antarctic	
antelope	s
antic	s
anticipate	d, ẹing, s
anticipation	s
antique	-dealer, -shop, s
antirrhinum	s
antiseptic	s
antler	s
anvil	s
anxiet y	ies
anxious	ly
any	body, one, how, thing, way, where

ap	
apart	
apartment	s
ape	d, ẹing, s
apiar y	ies
apiece	
apologetic	al, ally
apologize	d, ẹing, s
apolog y	ies
apostle	s
appal	led, ling, lingly, s
apparatus	es or **apparatus**
apparent	ly
appeal	ed, ing, ingly, s
appear	ed, ing, ance, s
appendicitis	
appetite	s
appetizing	ly
applaud	ed, ing, s
applause	
apple	-core, -pie, -sauce, -tart, -tree, s
appliance	s
applicant	s
application	s
apply	ing
appl ied	ies
appoint	ed, ing, ment, s
appreciate	d, ẹing, s
appreciation	
apprentice	d, ẹing, ship, s
approach	ed, ing, es
approval	
approve	d, ẹing, s
approximate	ly, d, ẹing, s
apricot	s
April	-fool, s
apron	s

ẹ Drop **e** before adding *ing*

aq ar   as

aq

aquarium	s or **aquaria**
aquatic	s
aqueduct	s

ar

arable	
arc* (curve)	-lamp, -light, s
arcade	s
arch	ed, ing, es
archway	s
archaeological	ly
archaeologist	s
archaeology	
archer	y, s
architect	ure, ural, s
arctic	
are	
aren't (are not)	
area	s
arena	s
argue	d, ℮ing, s
argument	ative, s
arise	n, ℮ing, s
arithmetic	al
ark* (boat; box)	s
arm	ed, ing, band, chair, ful, hole, pit, s
armada	s
armament	s
armistice	s
armour	ed, y, -plated, -plating
arm y	ies
arose	
around	
arouse	d, ℮ing, s
arrange	d, ℮ing, r, ment, s

array	ed, ing, s
arrest	ed, ing, s
arrival	s
arrive	d, ℮ing, s
arrow	-head, s
arsenic	
art	work, s
artist	ic, ically, s
artful	ly, ness
arter y	ies
article	s
artificial	ity, ly, ness
artillery	man, men

as

ascend	ed, ing, s
ascent	s
ascertain	ed, ing, s
ash	en, y, es
ashamed	
ashore	
aside	
ask	ed, ing, s
asleep	
asparagus	
asphyxiate	d, ℮ing, s
aspirin	s
ass	es
assail	ed, ing, ant, s
assassin	ation, s
assassinate	d, ℮ing, s
assault	ed, ing, s
assemble	d, ℮ing, s
assembl y	ies
assist	ed, ing, ance, s
assistant	s

*℮ Drop **e** before adding ing*

*   arc
    ark

at

au av

associate	d, ɇing, s
association	s
assort	ed, ing, ment, s
assume	d, ɇing, s
assure	d, ɇing, s
aster	s
asthma	tic, tical
astonish	ed, ing, es, ment
astound	ed, ing, s
astray	
astride	
astrologer	s
astrolog y	ical
astronaut	s
astronomer	s
astronom y	ical
asylum	s

at

ate* (eat)	
athlete	s
athletic	ally, s
Atlantic	
atlas	es
atmosphere	s
atom	ic, -bomb, s
atrocious	ly, ness
attach	ed, ing, able, es
attachment	s
attack	ed, ing, er, s
attain	ed, ing, able, ment, s
attempt	ed, ing, s
attend	ed, ing, ance, s
attendant	s
attention	s
attentive	ly, ness

attic	s
attitude	s
attract	ed, ing, ion, s
attractive	ly, ness
attribute	d, ɇing, s

au

auburn	
auction	ed, ing, eer, s
audible	
audience	s
audition	ed, ing, s
August	s
aunt	s
auntie s or **aunt** y	ies
author	s
authoress	es
authorit y	ies
authorize	d, ɇing, s
autobiograph y	ical, ies
autograph	ed, ing, s
automatic	ally
automation	
autumn	al, s

av

available	
avalanche	s
avenge	d, ɇing, r, s
avenue	s
average	d, ɇing, s
aviar y	ies
aviation	
aviator	s
avoid	ed, ing, able, ance, s

ɇ Drop **e** before adding *ing*

  ate
 * eight (8)

aw ax ba

aw

await	ed, ing, s
awake	d, ǿing, s
awaken	ed, ing, s
award	ed, ing, s
aware	ness
away	
awe	some, struck, stricken
awful	ly, ness
awhile	
awkward	ly, ness
awning	s
awoke or **awaked**	
awry	

ax

axe	d, ǿing, -blade, -handle, s
ax is	es
axle	s

ba

babe	s
baboon	s
bab y	ies
bachelor	s
back	ed, ing, cloth, ground, yard, s
backward	ly, ness, s
bacon	
bad	-tempered, ly, ness
badge	s
badger	ed, ing, s
badminton	-racket
baffle	d, ǿing, s
bag	ged, ging, ful, -snatcher, s
baggage	

bagg y	ier, iest, ily, iness
bagpipe	s
bail* (wicket cross-piece)	s
bait	ed, ing, s
bake	d, ǿing, r, house, s
baker y	ies
balance	d, ǿing, r, s
balcon y	ies
bald	ing, er, est, ly, ness, -headed
bale* (bundle)	d, ǿing, r, s
bale* ⎰ out of plane or ⎱	d, ǿing, r, s
bail* ⎱ throw out water ⎰	ed, ing, er, s
ball*	-game, point, -pen, room, s
ballast	
ballerina	s
ballet	-dancing, -dancer, -shoe, s
balloon	ed, ing, ist, s
ballot	ed, ing, -paper, s
bamboo	s
ban	ned, ning, s
banana	s
band	ed, ing, sman, smen, stand, s
bandage	d, ǿing, s
bandit	s
bang	ed, ing, er, s
bangle	s
banish	ed, ing, es, ment
banister	s
banjo	es or s
bank	ed, ing, er, -book, note, s
bankrupt	ed, ing, s, cy
banner	s
banquet	ed, ing, s
bantam	s
baptism	s
baptize	d, ǿing, s
bar	red, ring, maid, s

*ǿ Drop **e** before adding ing*

*	bail	ball
	bale	bawl

be

barbecue	*d, ∅ing, s*
barbed	*-wire*
barber	*s*
bare* (naked; empty)	*ly, ness, d, ∅ing, s*
bargain	*ed, ing, er, s*
barge	*d, ∅ing, e, -pole, s*
bark	*ed, ing, er, s*
barley	*corn, -sugar, -water, s*
barn	*-dance, -owl, yard, s*
barnacle	*s*
barometer	*s*
baron* (lord)	*et, s*
barrack	*ed, ing, er, -room, -square, s*
barrel	*ful, s*
barren* (bare; empty)	*ly, ness*
barricade	*d, ∅ing, s*
barrier	*s*
barrister	*s*
barrow	*-boy, s*
barter	*ed, ing, er, s*
base	*d, ∅ing, r, st, ly, less, ness, -line, s*
baseball	*s*
basement	*s*
bash	*ed, ing, es*
bashful	*ly, ness*
basin	*ful, s*
bask	*ed, ing, s*
basket	*ball, ful, s*
bat	*ted, ting, sman, smen, s*
batch	*es*
bath	*ed, ing, mat, robe, room, -water, s*
bathe	*d, ∅ing, r, s*
bathing-costume	*s*
baton	*s*
battalion	*s*
batter	*ed, ing, s*
battery	*ies*

battle	*d, ∅ing, axe, field, ship, s*
bawl* (shout; cry out)	*ed, ing, s*
bay	*-window, s*
bayonet	*ed, ing, s*
bazaar	*s*

be

beach* (seashore)	*ed, ing, es*
beacon	*s*
bead	*ed, ing, work, s*
beak	*s*
beaker	*s*
beam	*ed, ing, s*
bean* (plant)	*-bag, pole, stalk, s*
bear* (carry; endure)	*able, ing, er, s*
bear* (animal)	*skin, s*
beard	*ed, s*
beast	*s*
beastly	*ier, iest, iness*
beat* (hit; defeat)	*en, ing, er, s*
beautiful	*ly*
beauty	*ies*
beaver	*s*
became	
because	
beckon	*ed, ing, s*
become	*∅ing, s*
bed	*ded, ding, clothes, side, time, room, s*
bee	*hive, line, keeper, s*
beech* (tree)	*es*
beef	*burger, eater, steak, s*
been* (past of be)	
beer	*y, -barrel, -bottle, -can, s*
beet* (vegetable)	*root, s*
beetle	*s*
before	*hand*

*∅ Drop **e** before adding *ing**

*	bare	baron	bawl	beach	bean	beat
	bear	barren	ball	beech	been	beet

bi

beg	ged, ging, s		**bi**	
beggar	ly, s	Bible	s	
began		bicker	ed, ing, s	
begin	ning, ner, s	bicycle	d, ėing, -clip, -pump, s	
begun		bid	ding, der, s	
begone		bide	d, ėing, s	
behave	d, ėing, s	big	ger, gest, ness	
behaviour		bike	d, ėing, s	
behead	ed, ing, s	bikini	s	
behind	hand	bilberr y	ies	
being	s	bilge	-water, -pump, s	
belief	s	bilious	ly, ness	
believe	d, ėing, r, s	bill	ed, ing, s	
bell	-ringer, -tent, -tower, s	billet	ed, ing, s	
bellow	ed, ing, er, s	billiard	-ball, -cue, -room, -table, s	
belong	ed, ing, s	billion	s	
below		billow	ed, ing, s	
belt	ed, ing, s	bind	ing, er, s	
bench	es	bingo	-hall, s	
bend	ing, er, s	binoculars		
bent		biograph y	ical, ies	
beneath		biolog y	ical, ist	
benefit	ed, ing, s	biped	s	
benevolent	ly	birch	es	
beret* (cap)	s	bird	-bath, -cage, -seed, -table, s	
berry* (fruit)	ies	birth* (born)	day, mark, place, rate, s	
berth* (bunk; moor a ship)	ed, ing, s	biscuit	s	
beside	s	bisect	ed, ing, ion, s	
besiege	d, ėing, r, s	bishop	s	
best	-seller	bison	bison	
bet	ted, ting, ter, s	bit	ty, s	
betray	al, ed, ing, er, s	bitch	es	
better	ed, ing, s	bite	ėing, r, s	
between		bitten		
beware		bitter	er, est, ly, ness	
bewilder	ed, ing, ment, s	bittern	s	
beyond		bivouac	ked, king, s	

ė Drop **e** before adding *ing*

* beret   berth
berry   birth
bury

bl   bo

bl

black	ed, ing, er, est, ness, smith, s
black	-beetle, bird, board, -currant, s
blackberry	ing
blackberr ied	ies
blacken	ed, ing, s
blackmail	ed, ing, er, s
blade	d, s
blame	d, ǿing, less, s
blancmange	s
blank	ed, ing, er, est, ly, ness, s
blanket	s
blare	d, ǿing, s
blast	ed, ing, s
blaze	d, ǿing, s
blazer	s
bleach	ed, ing, es
bleak	er, est, ly, ness
bleat	ed, ing, s
bleed	ing, s
bled	
blend	ed, ing, er, s
bless	ed, ing, ings, es
blew* (blow)	
blind	ed, ing, er, est, ly, ness, s
blindfold	ed, ing, s
blind-man's-buff	
blink	ed, ing, er, s
blister	ed, ing, s
blizzard	s
block	age, ed, ing, s
blockade	d, ǿing, s
blond (masc.)	er, est, s
blonde (fem.)	r, st, s
blood	hound, shed, -stained, thirsty, y
bloom	ed, ing, s
blossom	ed, ing, s

blot	ted, ting, ter, s
blouse	s
blow	n, ing, y, er, lamp, pipe, s
blue* (colour)	r, st, ness, bell, bottle, s
blunder	ed, ing, s
blunt	ed, ing, er, est, ly, ness, s
blush	ed, ing, es
bluster	ed, ing, y, s

bo

boar* (male pig)	s
board* (wood; ship; lodge)	ed, ing, s
boarder* (one who boards; lodger)	s
boast	ed, ing, er, s
boastful	ly, ness
boat	ed, ing, er, man, men, -race, s
bob	bed, bing, -sleigh, s
bod y	ies
bog	ged, ging, s
bogg y	ier, iest, iness
boil	ed, ing, er, s
boisterous	ly, ness
bold	er,* est, ly, ness
bolt	ed, ing, s
bomb	ed, ing, er, -proof, shell, sight, s
bombard	ed, ing, ment, s
bone	d, ǿing, ǿy, -dry, -idle, -shaker, s
bonfire	s
bonnet	s
bonn y	ier, iest, ily, iness
book	ed, ing, case, let, seller, stall, s
booking office	s
boom	ed, ing, s
boot	ed, ing, lace, s
border* (edge)	ed, ing, er, less, line, s
bore* (drill hole; weary)	d,* ǿing, dom, s

ǿ Drop **e** before adding ing

*	blew	boar	board	boarder	bolder
	blue	bore	bored	border	boulder

born* (birth)	
borne* (carried)	
borrow	ed, ing, er, s
boss	ed, ing, es
boss y	ier, iest, ily, iness
botan y	ical, ist
both	
bother	ed, ing, some, s
bottle	d, ∉ing, -opener, s
bottom	ed, ˙ing, less, s
bough* (branch)	s
bought (buy)	
boulder* (large rock)	s
bounce	d, ∉ing, r, s
bound	ed, ing, less, s
boundar y	ies
bouquet	s
bow* (bend)	ed, ing, s
bow	man, men, shot, string, -tie, s
bowl	ed, ing, er, s
bowl	ful, s
box	ed, ing, es
boxer	s
Boxing Day	s
boy* (lad)	ish, hood, -friend, s
Boy Scout	s

br

brace	d, ∉ing, s
bracelet	s
bracken	
bracket	ed, ing, s
brag	ged, ging, gart, s
braid	ed, ing, s
brain	ed, ing, less, storm, wave, s
brain y	ier, iest, ily, iness

brake* (to stop)	d, ∉ing, s
bramble	s
branch	ed, ing, es
brand	ed, ing, -new, s
brandish	ed, ing, es
brand y	ies
brass	es
brave	d, ∉ing, r, st, ly, s
bravery	
bravo	s
brawl	ed, ing, er, s
brawn	
brawn y	ier, iest, iness
brazen	ed, ing, ly, ness
brazier	s
bread*	-bin, -board, -sauce, -crumb, s
breadth	s
break*	able, age, ing, er, -down, water, s
breakfast	ed, ing, -table, -room, s
breast	ed, ing, plate, stroke, s
breath	less, lessly, -taking, s
breathe	d, ∉ing, r, s
bred* (brought-up)	
breed	ing, er, s
breeze	s
breez y	ier, iest, ily, iness
brew	ed, ing, er, s
brewer y	ies
bribe	d, ∉ing, ry, s
brick	ed, ing, laying, layer, work, yard, s
bridal* (of a bride, wedding)	-gown
bride	groom, smaid, s
bridge	d, ∉ing, head, s
bridle* (horse's headgear)	-path, road, s
brief	ed, ing, er, est, ly, ness, case, s
brigade	s
brigand	s

∉ Drop **e** before adding *ing*

*							
	born	bough	boulder	boy	brake	bread	bridal
	borne	bow	bolder	buoy	break	bred	bridle

bright	er, est, ly, ness
brighten	ed, ing, s
brilliance	
brilliant	ly
brim	med, ming, ful, s
bring	ing, s
brink	s
brisk	er, est, ly, ness
bristle	d, ėing, s
bristly	ier, iest, iness
brittle	ness
broad	er, est, ly, minded, side, s
broaden	ed, ing, s
broadcast	ing, er, s
brocade	s
broccoli	
broke	
broken	-down, -hearted
bronchitis	
bronze	d, ėing, s
brooch	es
brood	ed, ing, y, s
brook	s
broom	stick, s
broth	s
brother	ly, s
brother(s)**-in-law**	
brought (bring)	
brow	s
brown	ed, ing, er, est, ish, ness, s
brownie	s
bruise	d, ėing, r, s
brunette	s
brush	ed, ing, es
Brussels sprouts	
brutal	ity, ly
brute	s

bu

bubble	d, ėing, -bath, -gum, s
bubbly	ier, iest, iness
buccaneer	s
buck	ed, ing, skin, s
bucket	ful, s
buckle	d, ėing, s
bud	ded, ding, s
budge	d, ėing, s
budgerigar	s
budget	ed, ing, s
buffalo	es or **buffalo**
buffer	s
buffet	ed, ing, s
bugle	-call, r, s
build	ing, er, s
built	
bulb	s
bulge	d, ėing, s
bulk	
bulky	ier, iest, ily, iness
bull	dog, fight, frog, ring, -terrier, s
bull's-eye	s
bulldoze	d, ėing, r, s
bullet	-hole, -proof, -wound, s
bulletin	s
bullion	
bullock	s
bully	ing
bullied	ies
bulrush	es
bumble-bee	s
bump	ed, ing, er, s
bumpy	ier, iest, ily, iness
bunch	ed, ing, es
bundle	d, ėing, s
bung	ed, ing, -hole, s

ė Drop **e** before adding ing

bungalow	s
bungle	d, e̸ing, r, s
bunk	s
bunker	ed, ing, s
Bunsen burner	s
bunting	
buoy* (floating marker)	ant, ed, ing, s
burden	ed, ing, some, s
bureau	x or s
burglar	-alarm, s
burglar y	ies
burgle	d, e̸ing, s
burial	-ground, -place, s
burl y	ier, iest, ily, iness
burn	ed, ing, er, s
burnt or burned	
burrow	ed, ing, er, s
burst	ing, s
bury* (cover)	ing
bur ied	ies
bus	man, men, es
busb y	ies
bush	es
bush y	ier, iest, ily, iness
business	man, men, es
bustle	d, e̸ing, r, s
busy	ing, ness
bus ied	ier, iest, ily, ies
butcher	ed, ing, s
butler	s
butter	ed, ing, scotch, cup, s
butterfl y	ies
button	ed, ing, -hole, s
buy* (purchase)	ing, er, s
buzz	ed, ing, es
buzzer	s
buzzard	s

by

by* (near to, etc.)	
bye* (a run)	s
bygone	s
by-pass	ed, ing, es
bystander	s
byway	s

ca

cabaret	s
cabbage	s
cabin	-boy, s
cabinet	-maker, s
cable	d, e̸ing, gram, -car, s
cackle	d, e̸ing, r, s
cactus	es or cacti
caddie* (golfer's club-carrier)	d, s
caddying	
cadd y* (tea box)	ies
cadet	s
cadge	d, e̸ing, r, s
café	s
cafeteria	s
cage	d, e̸ing, s
cake	d, e̸ing, s
calamit y	ies
calculate	d, e̸ing, s
calculation	s
calculator	s
calendar	s
calf	skin, calves
call	ed, ing, er, s
calm	ed, ing, er, est, ly, ness, s
came	
camel	-hair, s
camera	man, men, s
camouflage	d, e̸ing, s

e̸ Drop **e** before adding *ing*

*	buoy	bury	buy	caddie
	boy	beret	bye	caddy
		berry	by	

camp *ed, ing, er, -bed, -fire, site, s*	**career** *ed, ing, s*
campaign *ed, ing, er, s*	**caress** *ed, ing, es*
canal *s*	**cargo** *es*
canary *ies*	**caricature** *d, ꬿing, s*
cancel *led, ling, lation, s*	**carnation** *s*
candidate *s*	**carnival** *s*
candle *-light, wick, stick, s*	**carnivorous**
candy *ied, ies*	**carol** *led, ling, ler, -singer, s*
cane *d, ꬿing, s*	**carpenter** *s*
cannibal *ism, s*	**carpentry**
cannon *ed, -ball, -shot, s* or **cannon**	**carpet** *ed, ing, -sweeper, s*
cannot	**carriage** *way, s*
can't (cannot)	**carrot** *s*
canoe *d, ing, ist, s*	**carry** *ing*
canteen *s*	**carr**ied *ies*
canter *ed, ing, s*	**carrier** *-bag, -pigeon, s*
canvas* (strong cloth) *es*	**cart** *ed, ing, -load, -horse, -wheel, s*
canvass* (seek votes, orders) *ed, ing, es*	**carton** *s*
canyon *s*	**cartoon** *ed, ing, ist, s*
capable *y*	**cartridge** *-belt, -case, s*
cape *s*	**carve** *d, ꬿing, r, s*
capital *s*	**cascade** *d, ꬿing, s*
capsize *d, ꬿing, s*	**case** *s*
capsule *s*	**cash** *ed, ing, -box, es*
captain *ed, ing, s*	**cashier** *s*
captive *s*	**cask** *s*
captivity *ies*	**casket** *s*
capture *d, ꬿing, s*	**casserole** *d, ꬿing, s*
car *-load, -park, port, s*	**cassette** *-player, -recorder, s*
caramel *s*	**cast** *ing, s*
caravan *ned, ning, ner, s*	**castaway** *s*
carcass es or **carcase** *s*	**castle** *s*
card *board, -game, -room, -table, s*	**castor oil**
cardigan *s*	**casual** *ly, ness, s*
care *d, ꬿing, free, taker, s*	**casualt**y *ies*
careful *ly, ness*	**catalogue** *d, ꬿing, s*
careless *ly, ness*	**catapult** *ed, ing, s*

ꬿ Drop **e** before adding *ing*

*   canvas
      canvass

ce

catastrophe	s
catch	ing, es
catchy	ier, iest, iness
cater	ed, ing, er, s
caterpillar	s
cathedral	s
Catherine wheel	s
Catholic	s
catkin	s
cattle	-market, -shed, -show, -truck
caught	
cauldron	s
cauliflower	s
cause	d, ∅ing, s
caution	ed, ing, s
cautious	ly, ness
cavalier	s
cavalry	
cave	d, ∅ing, -man, -men, -dweller, s
cavern	s
cavity	ies

ce

cease	d, ∅ing, less, lessly, s
cedar	s
ceiling* (roof of room)	s
celandine	s
celebrate	d, ∅ing, s
celebration	s
celebrity	ies
celery	
cell* (small room)	s
cellar* (underground room)	s
cello	s
cellophane	
cement	ed, ing, -mixer, s

cha

cemetery	ies
cent* (coin)	s
centigrade	
centimetre	s
central	ly
centre	d, ∅ing, -forward, -piece, s
century	ies
cereal* (wheat, oats, etc.)	s
ceremony	ies
certain	ly, ty
certificate	s

ch

chaffinch	es
chain	ed, ing, -mail, -saw, -store, s
chair	ed, ing, man, woman, -lift, s
chalet	s
chalk	ed, ing, s
chalky	ier, iest, iness
challenge	d, ∅ing, r, s
chamber	maid, s
chamois	-leather
champagne	s
champion	ed, ing, ship, s
chance	d, ∅ing, s
chandelier	s
change	able, d, ∅ing, s
channel	led, ling, s
chant	ed, ing, s
chaos	
chaotic	ally
chapel	s
chapter	s
char	red, ring, woman, women, s
character	istic, s
charade	s

∅ Drop **e** before adding *ing*

*	ceiling	cell	cellar	cent	cereal
	sealing	sell	seller	sent	serial
				scent	

charcoal		**chick**	*weed, s*	
charge	*d, ẻing, r, s*	**chicken**	*-feed, -wire, s* or **chicken**	
chariot	*eer, s*	**chicken-pox**		
charit *y*	*ies*	**chief**	*ly, tain, s*	
charm	*ed, ing, er, s*	**chilblain**	*s*	
chart	*ed, ing, room, s*	**child**	*ish, hood, like, less,* **children**	
charter	*ed, ing, s*	**chill**	*ed, ing, er, s*	
chase	*d, ẻing, r, s*	**chill** *y*	*ier, iest, ily, iness*	
chasm	*s*	**chime**	*d, ẻing, s*	
chat	*ted, ting, s*	**chimney** *-pot. -stack, -sweep, s*		
chatter	*ed, ing, er, s*	**chimpanzee**	*s*	
chatt *y*	*ier, iest, ily, iness*	**chin**	*-strap, s*	
chauffeur	*s*	**china**	*-shop, ware*	
cheap	*er, est, ly, ness*	**chink**	*ed, ing, s*	
cheapen	*ed, ing, s*	**chintz**	*es*	
cheat	*ed, ing, er, s*	**chip**	*ped, ping, per, s*	
check*	*ed, ing, er, -list, -out, -point, s*	**chirp**	*ed, ing, s*	
check* (pattern)	*ed, s*	**chirp** *y*	*ier, iest, ily, iness*	
cheek	*ed, ing, -bone, s*	**chisel**	*led, ling, s*	
cheek *y*	*ier, iest, ily, iness*	**chivalrous**	*ly*	
cheer	*ed, ing, -leader, s*	**chivalry**		
cheerful	*ly, ness*	**chlorine**		
cheerless	*ly, ness*	**chloroform**	*ed, ing, s*	
cheer *y*	*ier, iest, ily, iness*	**chocolate**	*s*	
cheese	*burger, cake, cloth, -straw, s*	**choice**	*r, st, ly, ness, s*	
chef	*s*	**choir*** (of singers)	*-boy, -master, s*	
chemical	*ly, s*	**choke**	*d, ẻing, s*	
chemist	*s*	**choose**	*ẻing, s*	
chemistry		**chose**	*n*	
cheque* (money-order)	*-book, s*	**chop**	*ped, ping, per, s*	
cherish	*ed, ing, es*	**chopstick**	*s*	
cherr *y*	*ies*	**chorus**	*ed, ing, es*	
chess	*-board, -piece, -man, -men*	**chow**	*s*	
chest	*s*	**christen**	*ed, ing, s*	
chestnut	*-tree, s*	**Christ**		
chew	*ed, ing, y, er, s*	**Christian**	*ity, s*	
chewing-gum		**Christmas**	*-box, es, -time, -tree, sy*	

ẻ Drop **e** before adding *ing*

*	check
	cheque

choir
quire

chromium	*-plated, -plating*
chrysalis	*es*
chrysanthemum	*s*
chubb y	*ier, iest, ily, iness*
chuckle	*d, ẹing, s*
chug	*ged, ging, s*
chum	*med, ming, s*
chumm y	*ier, iest, ily, iness*
chunk	*s*
church	*es*
churchyard	*s*
churn	*ed, ing, s*
chute* (a slide)	*s*
chutney	*s*

ci

cider or **cyder**	*s*
cigar	*-case, -holder, -lighter, s*
cigarette	*-case, -holder, -lighter, s*
cinder	*-path, -track, s*
cine-	*camera, film, projector*
cinema	*-goer, s*
circle	*d, ẹing, s*
circular	*s*
circulate	*d, ẹing, s*
circulation	*s*
circumference	*s*
circumstance	*s*
circus	*es*
cistern	*s*
citizen	*s*
cit y	*ies*
civil	*ity, ly*
civilian	*s*
civilization	*s*
civilize	*d, ẹing, s*

cl

claim	*ed, ing, s*
clamber	*ed, ing, s*
clamm y	*ier, iest, ily, iness*
clamp	*ed, ing, s*
clang	*ed, ing, s*
clank	*ed, ing, s*
clap	*ped, ping, per, s*
clash	*ed, ing, es*
clasp	*ed, ing, s*
class	*ed, ing, es, rooms*
classic	*al, s*
clatter	*ed, ing, s*
claw	*ed, ing, s*
clay	*ey, -pigeon, -pipe, -pit, s*
clean	*ed, ing, er, est, ly, ness, s*
cleanliness	
cleanse	*d, ẹing, r, s*
clear	*ed, ing, er, est, ly, ness, s*
clench	*ed, ing, es*
clergy	*man, men*
clerk	*s*
clever	*er, est, ly, ness*
click	*ed, ing, s*
client	*s*
cliff	*-top, s*
climate	*s*
climb	*ed, ing, er, s*
cling	*ing, s*
clinic	*al, ally, s*
clink	*ed, ing, er, s*
clip	*ped, ping, per, s*
cloak	*ed, ing, room, s*
clock	*ed, ing, wise, work, -tower, s*
cloister	*ed, ing, s*
close (shut)	*d, ẹing, s*
close (near; stuffy)	*r, st, ly, ness*

*ẹ Drop **e** before adding ing*

* chute / shoot

COa   cob   coc   cod   cof   coi   col   com

cloth	s
clothe	d, ẹing, s
clothes	-basket, -horse, -line, -peg
cloud	ed, ing, less, lessly, burst, s
cloud y	ier, iest, ily, iness
clover	s
clown	ed, ing, s
club	bed, bing, house, room, s
cluck	ed, ing, s
clue	less, s
clump	ed, ing, s
clums y	ier, iest, ily, iness
clung	
cluster	ed, ing, s
clutch	ed, ing, es
clutter	ed, ing, s

co

coach	man, men, ed, ing, es
coal	man, men, -mine, -miner, s
coarse* (rough)	r, st, ly, ness
coast	al, ed, ing, line, guard, s
coat	ed, ing, -hanger, s
coax	ed, ing, es
cobble	d, ẹing, r, -stone, s
cobra	s
cobweb	by, s
cock	ed, ing, -fight, pit, tail, s
cockatoo	s
cockerel	s
cockle	-shell, s
cockney	s
cockroach	es
cocoa	
coconut	-matting, -milk, -palm, s
cocoon	s

code	d, ẹing, s
coffee	-bar, -bean, -cup, -pot, -table, s
coffin	s
coil	ed, ing, s
coin	age, ed, ing, s
coincide	d, ẹing, s
coincidence	s
cold	er, est, ish, ly, ness, -storage, s
collapse	d, ẹing, s
collapsible	
collar	-bone, -stud, s
collect	ed, ing, ion, or, s
college	s
collide	d, ẹing, s
collision	s
collie	s
collier	s
collier y	ies
colonel* (officer)	s
colonize	d, ẹing, s
colon y	ies
colossal	ly
colour	ed, ing, ful, less, -scheme, s
column	s
comb	ed, ing, s
combat	ed, ing, s
combination	s
combine	d, ẹing, -harvester, s
come	ẹing, s
comedian (masc.)	s
comedienne (fem.)	s
comed y	ies
comet	s
comfort	able, ably, ed, ing, s
comic	al, ally, s
command	ed, ing, er, ment, s
commemorate	d, ẹing, s

ẹ Drop **e** before adding *ing*

*	coarse	colonel
	course	kernel

commence	*d, ɇing, ment, s*	**conceal**	*ed, ing, ment, s*
comment	*ed, ing, ator, s*	**conceit**	*ed, edly*
commentar y	*ies*	**concentrate**	*d, ɇing, s*
commerce		**concentration**	
commercial	*s*	**concern**	*ed, ing, s*
commission	*ed, ing, aire, er, s*	**concert**	*s*
commit	*ted, ting, ment, s*	**conclude**	*d, ɇing, s*
committee	*-room, s*	**conclusion**	*s*
common	*er, est, ly, ness, -room, s*	**concrete**	*d, ɇing, s*
commotion	*s*	**condemn**	*ed, ing, ation, s*
communicate	*d, ɇing, s*	**condition**	*ed, ing, er, s*
communication	*s*	**conduct**	*ed, ing, or, s*
communion		**conductress**	*es*
communit y	*ies*	**conference**	*s*
compact	*s*	**confess**	*ed, ing, es*
companion	*ship, s*	**confession**	*s*
compan y	*ies*	**confetti**	
comparative	*ly, s*	**confide**	*d, ɇing, s*
compare	*d, ɇing, s*	**confidence**	
comparison	*s*	**confident**	*ial, ially, ly*
compartment	*s*	**confirm**	*ed, ing, ation, s*
compass	*es*	**confiscate**	*d, ɇing, s*
compel	*led, ling, s*	**confuse**	*d, ɇing, s*
compete	*d, ɇing, s*	**confusion**	*s*
competition	*s*	**congratulate**	*d, ɇing, s*
competitor	*s*	**congratulation**	*s*
complain	*ed, ing, s*	**congregate**	*d, ɇing, s*
complaint	*s*	**congregation**	*s*
complete	*d, ɇing, ly, ness, s*	**conjure**	*d, ɇing, s*
complexion	*s*	**conjurer** or **conjuror**	*s*
complicate	*d, ɇing, s*	**conker*** (horse-chestnut)	*s*
compliment	*ed, ing, ary, s*	**connect**	*ed, ing, ion, s*
compose	*d, ɇing, r, s*	**conquer*** (defeat)	*ed, ing, or, s*
composition	*s*	**conquest**	*s*
comprehensive school	*s*	**conscience**	*-smitten, s*
computer	*s*	**conscientious**	*ly, ness*
comrade	*ship, s*	**conscious**	*ly, ness*

ɇ Drop **e** before adding *ing*

* conker
conquer

consent	*ed, ing, s*	**cook**	*ed, ing, er, ery, book, house, s*	
consequence	*s*	**cool**	*ed, ing, er, est, ish, ly, ness, s*	
consequent	*ly*	**co-operate**	*d, ǿing, s*	
conservative	*s*	**co-operation**		
consider	*ed, ing, able, ably, ate, ation, s*	**copper**	*s*	
consist	*ed, ing, s*	**coppice** or **copse**	*s*	
consolation	*-prize, s*	**copy**	*ing*	
conspicuous	*ly, ness*	**cop** *ied*	*ies*	
constable	*s*	**coral**	*-island, -reef, s*	
constant	*ly*	**cord**	*s*	
construct	*ed, ing, ion, or, s*	**cordial**	*s*	
consult	*ed, ing, ation, s*	**cordon**	*ed, ing, s*	
consume	*d, ǿing, r, s*	**corduroy**	*s*	
contact	*ed, ing, s*	**core*** (middle of apple, etc.)	*d, ǿing, s*	
contain	*ed, ing, er, s*	**corgi**	*s*	
.contemporar *y*	*ies*	**cork**	*ed, ing, screw, s*	
content	*ed, ing, ment, s*	**corn**	*-cob, field, flake, s*	
contest	*ed, ing, ant, s*	**corned beef**		
continent	*al, s*	**corner**	*ed, ing, s*	
continual	*ly*	**cornet**	*s*	
continue	*d, ǿing, s*	**coronation**	*s*	
continuation		**corporal**	*s*	
continuous	*ly, ness*	**corporation**	*s*	
contradict	*ed, ing, ion, s*	**corps*** (group of cadets, etc.)	**corps**	
contribute	*d, ǿing, s*	**corpse**	*s*	
contribution	*s*	**correct**	*ed, ing, ion, ly, ness, s*	
control	*led, ling, ler, -column, -lever, s*	**correspond**	*ed, ing, ence, ent, s*	
convalesce	*d, ǿing, nce, nt, s*	**corridor**	*s*	
convenience	*s*	**cosmetic**	*s*	
convenient	*ly*	**cosmonaut**	*s*	
convent	*s*	**cost**	*ing, s*	
conversation	*s*	**costl** *y*	*ier, iest, iness*	
convert	*ed, ing, s*	**coster**	*monger, s*	
convey	*ed, ing, ance, s*	**costume**	*s*	
convict	*ed, ing, ion, s*	**cos** *y*	*ier, iest, ily, iness, ies*	
convince	*d, ǿing, s*	**cottage**	*s*	
convoy	*ed, ing, s*	**cotton**	*wool, s*	

*ǿ Drop **e** before adding* ing

* core
    corps

couch	*es*
cough	*ed, ing, er, -drop, -mixture, s*
could	
couldn't (could not)	
council	*lor, -chamber, -house, s*
count	*ed, ing, er, less, -down, s*
counter	*ed, ing, -attack, foil, s*
countess	*es*
country	*ies*
county	*ies*
couple	*d, ∉ing, s*
coupon	*s*
courage	
courageous	*ly, ness*
course* (track; direction; of course)	*s*
court	*ed, ing, ier, room, ship, yard, s*
courtesy	*ies*
cousin	*ly, s*
cove	*s*
cover	*ed, ing, s*
cow	*boy, hand, herd, hide, shed, s*
coward	*s*
cowardice	
cowardly	*iness*
cowslip	*s*

cr

crab	*-apple, -pot, s*
crack	*ed, ing, er, s*
crackle	*d, ∉ing, s*
cradle	*d, ∉ing, s*
craft	*sman, smen, s*
crafty	*ier, iest, ily, iness*
cram	*med, ming, mer, s*
cramp	*ed, ing, s*
crane	*d, ∉ing, -driver, s*

crank	*ed, ing, s*
crash	*ed, ing, es*
crate	*d, ∉ing, ful, s*
crater	*s*
crave	*d, ∉ing, s*
crawl	*ed, ing, er, s*
crayon	*ed, ing, s*
craze	*d, ∉ing, s*
crazy	*ier, iest, ily, iness*
creak* (noise)	*ed, ing, s*
creaky	*ier, iest, ily, iness*
cream	*ed, ing, er, -cake, -cheese, s*
creamy	*ier, iest, ily, iness*
crease	*d, ∉ing, s*
create	*d, ∉ing, s*
creature	*s*
credit	*able, ed, ing, or, s*
creek* (small bay, sea-coast inlet)	*s.*
creep	*ing, er, s*
creepy	*ier, iest, ily, iness*
cremate	*d, ∉ing, s*
crematorium	*s*
creosote	*d, ∉ing, s*
crept	
crescent	*s*
crest	*ed, ing, fallen, s*
crevice	*s*
crew	*ed, ing, s*
crib	*bed, bing, ber, s*
cricket	*ing, er, -field, s*
cried	
crier	*s*
cries	
crime	*s*
criminal	*s*
crimson	*ed, ing, s*
cringe	*d, ∉ing, s*

*∉ Drop **e** before adding ing*

crinkle	*d, ǿing, s*		**crumple**	*d, ǿing, s*
crinkl *y*	*ier, iest, iness*		**crunch**	*ed, ing, es*
cripple	*d, ǿing, s*		**crusade**	*d, ǿing, r, s*
crisp	*ed, ing, er, est, ly, ness, s*		**crush**	*ed, ing, es*
crisp *y*	*ier, iest, ily, iness*		**crust**	*s*
critic	*al, ally, ism, s*		**crust** *y*	*ier, iest, ily, iness*
criticize	*d, ǿing, s*		**crutch**	*es*
croak	*ed, ing, er, s*		**cry**	*ing*
croak *y*	*ier, iest, ily, iness*		**cr** *ied*	*ies*
crochet	*ed, ing, -hook, s*		**crypt**	*s*
crockery			**crystal**	*s*
crocodile	*s*			
crocus	*es*			
crook	*s*		**cu**	
crooked	*ly, ness*		**Cub Scout**	*s*
crop	*ped, ping, per, s*		**cube**	*d, ǿing, s*
croquet			**cubicle**	*s*
cross	*ed, ing, er, est, ly, ness, es*		**cuckoo**	*-clock, s*
crossroad	*s*		**cucumber**	*s*
crossword	*s*		**cuddle**	*d, ǿing, some, s*
crouch	*ed, ing, es*		**cue*** (hint; billiard-stick)	*s*
crow	*ed, ing, bar, s*		**cuff**	*-link, s*
crowd	*ed, ing, s*		**cul-de-sac**	**culs-de-sac**
crown	*ed, ing, s*		**culprit**	*s*
crucify	*ing*		**cultivate**	*d, ǿing, s*
crucif *ied*	*ies*		**cultivation**	
crucifix	*es*		**cunning**	*ly*
crucifixion	*s*		**cup**	*ful, s*
crude	*r, st, ly, ness*		**cupboard**	*s*
cruel	*ler, lest, ly*		**curate**	*s*
cruelt *y*	*ies*		**curator**	*s*
cruet	*s*		**curb*** (hold back)	*ed, ing, s*
cruise	*d, ǿing, r, s*		**curdle**	*d, ǿing, s*
crumb	*s*		**cure**	*d, ǿing, s*
crumble	*d, ǿing, s*		**curio**	*s*
crumbl *y*	*ier, iest, iness*		**curiosit** *y*	*ies*
crumpet	*s*		**curious**	*ly, ness*

ǿ Drop **e** *before adding* *ing*

*	cue	curb
	queue	kerb

curl	ed, ing, er, s
curl y	ier, iest, ily, iness
currant* (fruit)	-bread, -bun, -cake, s
current* (flow of water, air, etc.)	s
curr y	ied, ies
curse	d, ǿing, s
curt	ly, ness
curtain	ed, ing, s
curtsy	ing
curts ied	ies
curve	d, ǿing, s
cushion	s
custard	-powder, -pie, s
custom	s
customer	s
cut	ting, ter, -price, -rate, -throat, s
cutlass	es
cutlery	

cy

cycle	d, ǿing, -clip, s
cyclist	s
cyclone	s
cygnet* (young swan)	s
cylinder	s
cymbal	ist, s
cypress	es

da

dab	bed, bing, ber, s
dabble	d, ǿing, r, s
dachshund	s
dad	s
dadd y	ies
daffodil	s

daft	er, est, ly, ness
dagger	s
dahlia	s
dail y	ies
daint y	ier, iest, ily, iness, ies
dair y	ies
dais y	ies
dale	s
Dalmatian	s
dam	med, ming, s
damage	d, ǿing, s
dame	s
damp	ed, ing, er, est, ly, ness, s
dampen	ed, ing, er, s
damson	-tree, s
dance	d, ǿing, r, -band, -floor, s
dandelion	s
danger	s
dangerous	ly
dangle	d, ǿing, s
dank	er, est, ly, ness
dapple	d, ǿing, -grey, s
dare	d, ǿing, -devil, s
dark	er, est, ly, ness
darken	ed, ing, s
darling	s
darn	ed, ing, er, s
dart	ed, ing, -board, s
dash	ed, ing, es
date	d, ǿing, -stamp, -palm, s
daub	ed, ing, er, s
daughter	s
dawdle	d, ǿing, r, s
dawn	ed, ing, s
day	break, dream, light, time, s
daze	d, ǿing, s
dazzle	d, ǿing, r, s

ǿ Drop **e** before adding *ing*

*	currant	cygnet
	current	signet

de

de	
dead	-beat, -end, -heat, line, lock, ness
deaden	ed, ing, er, s
deadly	ier, iest, iness
deaf	-aid, er, est, ly, ness
deafen	ed, ing, s
deal	ing, er, s
dealt	
dear* (beloved; costly)	er, est, ly, ness, s
death	ly, -bed, -blow, -rate, -ray, -trap, s
debate	d, ẹing, r, s
debris	
debt	or, s
decay	ed, ing, s
deceit	ful, fully, s
deceive	d, ẹing, r, s
December	s
decent	ly
decide	d, dly, ẹing, s
decimal	s
decipher	ed, ing, s
decision	s
deck	ed, ing, -chair, s
declare	d, ẹing, s
decline	d, ẹing, s
decorate	d, ẹing, s
decoration	s
decorator	s
decrease	d, ẹing, s
deduct	ed, ing, ion, s
deed	s
deep	er, est, ly, ness
deepen	ed, ing, s
deer* (animal)	skin, stalker, -park, **deer**
defeat	ed, ing, s
defect	ive, s
defence	less, lessly, s

defend	ed, ing, er, s
defiant	ly
definite	ly
degree	s
delay	ed, ing, s
deliberate	ly, ness, d, ẹing, s
delicacy	ies
delicate	ly, ness
delicious	ly, ness
delight	ed, ing, s
delightful	ly, ness
deliver	ed, ing, ance, s
delivery	ies
deluge	d, ẹing, s
demand	ed, ing, s
demolish	ed, ing, es
demon	s
demonstrate	d, ẹing, s
demonstration	s
demonstrator	s
dense	r, st, ly, ness
dent	ed, ing, s
dentist	s
deny	ing
denied	ies
depart	ed, ing, ure, s
department	s
depend	ed, ing, able, ent, s
deport	ed, ing, ation, s
deposit	ed, ing, or, s
depot	s
depth	-charge, s
deputy	ies
derail	ed, ing, ment, s
derelict	s
descant	-recorder, s
descend	ed, ing, ant, s

ẹ Drop **e** before adding *ing*

* dear
  deer

di

descent	s		**di**	
describe	d, ẹing, s	**diagram**	s
description	s	**dial**	led, ling, ler, s
desert (sandy place)	s	**dialect**	s
desert* (run away)	ed, ing, ion, er, s	**dialogue**	s
deserve	d, ẹing, s	**diameter**	s
design	ed, ing, er, s	**diamond**	s
desire	d, ẹing, s	**diar** y	ies
desk	s	**dictate**	d, ẹing, s
desolate	d, ẹing, ly, ness, s	**dictation**	s
despair	ed, ing, ingly, s	**dictionar** y	ies
despatch or **dispatch**	ed, ing, es	**didn't** (did not)	
desperate	ly, ness	**die*** (small spotted cube)	**dice**
desperation		**die*** (lose life)	s
despise	d, ẹing, s	**died*** (lost life)	
despite		**dying*** (losing life)	
dessert* (fruit, pudding, etc.)	-spoon, s	**diet**	ed, ing, ician, s
destination	s	**differ**	ed, ing, ence, s
destroy	ed, ing, er, s	**different**	ly
destruction		**difficult**	
destructive	ly, ness	**difficult** y	ies
detach	ed, ing, es	**dig**	ging, ger, s
detail	ed, ing, s	**digest**	ed, ing, ion, ive, s
detain	ed, ing, s	**dignif** y	ied, ies
detect	ed, ing, ion, or, s	**dignity**	
detective	s	**dike** or **dyke**	s
detention	s	**dilapidated**	
determination		**dilute**	d, ẹing, s
determine	d, ẹing, s	**dim**	med, ming, mer, mest, ly, ness, s
detest	able, ed, ing, s	**dimension**	s
develop	ed, ing, er, ment, s	**dimple**	d, ẹing, s
device	s	**dine**	d, ẹing, r, s
devil	ish, ry, ment, s	**dining**	-car, -hall, -room, -table
devise	d, ẹing, s	**dingh** y	ies
devote	d, ẹing, s	**ding** y	ier, iest, ily, iness
devour	ed, ing, er, s	**dinner**	-hour, -service, -table, -time, s
dew* (moisture)	y, -drop, -fall, -pond, s	**dinosaur**	s

*ẹ Drop **e** before adding ing*

*	desert	dew	die	died	dying
	dessert	due	dye	dyed	dyeing
		Jew			

dip	*ped, ping, per, s*	**dismal**	*ly, ness*
diploma	*s*	**dismantle**	*d, ∉ing, s*
direct	*ed, ing, ly, ness, ive, or, s*	**dismay**	*ed, ing, s*
direction	*-finder, s*	**dismiss**	*ed, ing, es*
director *y*	*ies*	**dismount**	*ed, ing, s*
dirt	*-track*	**disobedience**	
dirt *ied*	*ier, iest, ily, iness, ies*	**disobedient**	*ly*
dirty	*ing*	**disobey**	*ed, ing, s*
disable	*d, ∉ing, ment, s*	**disorder**	*ly, s*
disadvantage	*s*	**dispatch** or **despatch**	*ed, ing, es*
disagree	*able, d, ing, ment, s*	**dispensar** *y*	*ies*
disappear	*ed, ing, ance, s*	**dispense**	*d, ∉ing, r, s*
disappoint	*ed, ing, ment, s*	**display**	*ed, ing, s*
disarm	*ed, ing, ament, s*	**displease**	*d, ∉ing, s*
disarrange	*d, ∉ing, ment, s*	**dispute**	*d, ∉ing, s*
disaster	*s*	**disqualify**	*ing*
disastrous	*ly*	**disqualif** *ied*	*ies, ication*
disc or **disk**	*s*	**dissatisfy**	*ing*
discharge	*d, ∉ing, s*	**dissatisf** *ied*	*ies, action*
disciple	*s*	**dissolve**	*d, ∉ing, s*
discipline	*d, ∉ing, s*	**distance**	*s*
discontent	*ed, edly, ment, s*	**distant**	*ly*
discothèque or **disco**	*-club, -dancing, s*	**distinct**	*ion, ive, ly, ness*
discourage	*d, ∉ing, ment, s*	**distinguish**	*able, ed, ing, es*
discover	*ed, ing, er, s*	**distract**	*ed, ing, ion, s*
discover *y*	*ies*	**distress**	*ed, ing, es*
discuss	*ed, ing, es*	**disribute**	*d, ∉ing, s*
discussion	*s*	**district**	*s*
disease	*d, s*	**disturb**	*ed, ing, ance, s*
disgrace	*d, ∉ing, s*	**ditch**	*ed, ing, es*
disgraceful	*ly, ness*	**divan**	*s*
disguise	*d, ∉ing, s*	**dive**	*d, ∉ing, r, s*
disgust	*ed, ing, s*	**divert**	*ed, ing, s*
dish	*ed, ing, es*	**divide**	*d, ∉ing, r, s*
dishearten	*ed, ing, s*	**division**	*s*
dishonest	*ly, y*	**divorce**	*d, ∉ing, e, s*
dislike	*able, d, ∉ing, s*	**dizz** *y*	*ier, iest, ily, iness*

∉ Drop **e** before adding *ing*

do   dr

do			dr		
docile		*ly*	**drab**	*ber, best, ly, ness*	
dock	*ed, ing, er, yard, s*		**drag**	*ged, ging, -net, s*	
doctor		*˙ s*	**dragon**		*s*
document	*ed, ing, s*		**dragonfl** *y*		*ies*
dodge	*d, ∅ing, r, s*		**drain**	*age, ed, ing, -pipe, s*	
doe* (female animal)		*s*	**drake**		*s*
does			**drama**	*tic, tist, s*	
doesn't (does not)			**dramatize**	*d, ∅ing, s*	
doing		*s*	**drank**		
dole	*d, ∅ing, ful, fully, s*		**drape**	*d, ∅ing, s*	
doll		*s*	**draper**		*s*
dollar		*s*	**draper** *y*		*ies*
dolphin		*s*	**drastic**		*ally*
domestic		*ally, s*	**draught** *sman, smen, -board, s*		
domesticate	*d, ∅ing, s*		**draught** *y*	*ier, iest, ily, iness*	
domino		*es*	**draw**	*n, ing, er, s*	
donate	*d, ∅ing, s*		**drawbridge**		*s*
donation		*s*	**drawer**		*s*
done			**drawing** *-board, paper, -pin, -room, s*		
donkey		*s*	**dread**	*ed, ing, s*	
don't (do not)			**dreadful**	*ly, ness*	
doom	*ed, ing, sday, s*		**dream** *ed, ing, land, like, er, s*		
door *bell, keeper, mat, step, way, s*			**dreamt** or **dreamed**		
dormitor *y*		*ies*	**dream** *y*	*ier, iest, ily, iness*	
dose	*d, ∅ing, s*		**drear** *y*	*ier, iest, ily, iness*	
dot	*ted, ting, s*		**dredge**	*d, ∅ing, r, s*	
double *d, ∅ing, -jointed, -decker, s*			**drench**	*ed, ing, es*	
doubt	*ed, ing, less, er, s*		**dress**	*ed, ing, es*	
doubtful		*ly, ness*	**dresser**		*s*
dough* (moist flour) *boy, nut, y*			**dressing** *-gown, -case, -room, -table, s*		
douse or **dowse**	*d, ∅ing, s*		**dressmaker**		*s*
dove		*cote, s*	**drew**		
dowd *y*	*ier, iest, ily, iness*		**dribble**	*d, ∅ing, r, s*	
down *stairs, hill, fall, pour, ward, s*			**drift**	*ed, ing, er, s*	
doze	*d, ∅ing, s*		**drill**	*ed, ing, er, s*	
dozen	*s* or **dozen**		**drink**	*able, ing, er, s*	

*∅ Drop **e** before adding ing*

* doe
   dough

drip	*ped, ping, s*
drive	*éing, r, way, s*
driven	
drivel	*led, ling, ler, s*
drizzle	*d, éing, s*
drizzly	*ier, iest, iness*
dromedary	*ies*
drone	*d, éing, s*
droop	*ed, ing, s*
drop	*ped, ping, per, let, s*
drought	*s*
drove	
drown	*ed, ing, s*
drowse	*d, éing, s*
drowsy	*ier, iest, ily, iness*
drudgery	
drug	*ged, ging, gist, -addict, store, s*
drum	*med, ming, mer, -major, stick, s*
drunk	*ard, s*
drunken	*ly, ness*
dry	*ing, ness*
dried	*ier, iest, ies*
dryer or **drier** (noun)	*s*
dryly or **drily**	

du

dual* (two; double)	
duchess	*es*
duck	*ed, ing, ling, s*
due* (expected; owing)	*s*
duel* (a fight)	*led, ling, list, s*
duet	*s*
duffel or **duffle**	*-bag, -coat, s*
dug	*-out*
duke	*dom, s*
dull	*ed, ing, er, est, ish, y, ness, s*

duly	
dumb	*er, est, ly, ness*
dummy	*ies*
dump	*ed, ing, s*
dumpling	*s*
dunce	*s*
dungarees	
dungeon	*s*
duplicate	*d, éing, s*
durable	*ness*
duration	
during	
dusk	
dusky	*ier, iest, ily, iness*
dust	*ed, ing, man, men, bin, pan, er, s*
dusty	*ier, iest, ily, iness*
dutiful	*ly, ness*
duty	*ies*

dw

dwarf	*ed, ing, s* or **dwarves**
dwell	*ed, ing, er, s*
dwelling	*-house, -place, s*
dwelt or **dwelled**	
dwindle	*d, éing, s*

dy

dye* (colour)	*r, s*
dyed* (coloured)	
dyeing* (colouring)	
dying* (losing life)	
dyke or **dike**	*s*
dynamic	*al, ally, s*
dynamite	*d, éing, s*
dynamo	*s*

*é Drop **e** before adding ing*

*	due	dual		dye	dyed	dyeing
	dew	duel		die	died	dying
	Jew	jewel				

ea

each	
eager	ly, ness
eagle	t, s
ear	ache, -drum, phone, -plug, -ring, s
earwig	s
earl	dom, s
early	ier, iest, iness
earn* (be paid)	ed, ing, er, s
earnt or **earned**	
earnest	ly, ness
earth	quake, worm, work, s
earthen	ware
ease	d, ǿing, s
easy	ier, iest, ily, iness
easel	s
east	ern, erly, ward, wards
Easter	-egg, s
eat	able, en, ing, er s
eavesdrop	ped, ping, per, s

ec

eccentric	s
echo	ed, ing, es
éclair	s
eclipse	d, ǿing, s
economic	al, ally, s
economize	d, ǿing, s
economy	ies

ed

eddy	ing
eddied	ies
edge	d, ǿing, ways, wise, s
edible	

edit	ed, ing, s
edition	s
editor	ial, s
educate	d, ǿing, s
education	al, ally, alist, ist

ee

eel	s
eerie or **eer**y	ier, iest, ily, iness

ef

effect	ed, ing, s
effective	ly, ness
efficiency	
efficient	ly
effigy	ies
effort	less, lessly, s

eg

egg	-cup, -shell, -spoon, -timer, s

ei

eiderdown	s
either	

el

elaborate	d, ǿing, ly, ness, s
elapse	d, ǿing, s
elastic	ally, ity
elbow	ed, ing, s
elder	ly, s
eldest	
elect	ed, ing, ion, or, s

ǿ Drop **e** before adding *ing*

* earn
    urn

em

electric	al, ally, s
electrician	s
electricity	
electrocute	d, ȩing, s
elegant	ly
elephant	s
elevator	s
elf	in, ish, **elves**
eligible	
eliminate	d, ȩing, s
elimination	s
Elizabethan	s
elm	-tree, s
elocution	ist
elope	d, ȩing, ment, s
else	where

em

embankment	s
embark	ed, ing, ation, s
embarrass	ed, ing, es
embarrassment	s
emblem	s
embrace	d, ȩing, s
embroider	ed, ing, s
embroider y	ies
emerald	s
emerge	d, ȩing, s
emergenc y	ies
emigrate	d, ȩing, s
emperor	s
empire	s
employ	ed, ing, ment, ee, er, s
empress	es
empty	ing
empt ied	ier, iest, ily, iness, ies

en

en

enable	d, ȩing, s
enamel	led, ling, s
encamp	ed, ing, ment, s
enchant	ed, ing, ment, s
encircle	d, ȩing, ment, s
enclose	d, ȩing, s
enclosure	s
encore	d, ȩing, s
encounter	ed, ing, s
encourage	d, ȩing, ment, s
encyclop(a)edia	s
end	ed, ing, less, lessly, s
endanger	ed, ing, s
endeavour	ed, ing, s
endure	d, ȩing, s
endurance	s
enem y	ies
energetic	ally
energ y	ies
enforce	d, ȩing, ment, s
engage	d, ȩing, ment, s
engine	-driver, -room, s
engineer	ed, ing, s
engrave	d, ȩing, r, s
engulf	ed, ing, s
enjoy	able, ed, ing, ment, s
enlarge	d, ȩing, r, ment, s
enlist	ed, ing, ment, s
enormous	ly, ness
enough	
enquire or **inquire**	d, ȩing, r, s
enquir y or **inquir** y	ies
enrage	d, ȩing, s
enrol	led, ling, ment, s
entangle	d, ȩing, ment, s
enter	ed, ing, s

ȩ Drop **e** before adding *ing*

ep eq er   es ev

31

enterprise		s
entertain	ed, ing, ment, er, s	
enthusiasm		s
enthusiastic		ally
entire		ly, ness
entitle	d, ǿing, ment, s	
entrance		s
entry		ies
envelope		s
envious		ly, ness
environment	al, alist, s	
envy		ing
envied		ies

ep

epidemic	s
epilogue	s
episode	s

eq

equal	led, ling, ly, s
equalize	d, ǿing, r, s
equator	ial
equip	ped, ping, ment, s
equivalent	ly

er

erase	d, ǿing, r, s
erect	ed, ing, ion, s
err	ed, ing, ant, s
errand	s
erratic	ally
error	s
erupt	ed, ing, ion, s

es

escalator	s
escapade	s
escape	d, ǿing, r, s
escort	ed, ing, s
Eskimo	s or es or **Eskimo**
especial	ly
espionage	
esplanade	s
essay	ist, s
essence	s
essential	ly, s
establish	ed, ing, es
establishment	s
estate	s
estimate	d, ǿing, s
estuary	ies

ev

evacuate	d, ǿing, s
evacuation	s
evade	d, ǿing, s
evaporate	d, ǿing, s
eve	s
even	ed, ing, ly, ness, s
evening	s
event	ful, less, s
eventual	ly
ever	green, lasting, more
every	body, one, thing, where
evict	ed, ing, ion, s
evidence	s
evident	ly
evil	ly, ness, s
evolve	d, ǿing, s
evolution	s

ǿ Drop **e** before adding *ing*

ex

exact	*ly, ness*
exaggerate	*d, ẹing, s*
exaggeratior	*s*
examinatior	*s*
examine	*d, ẹing, r, s*
example	*s*
exasperate	*d, ẹing, s*
excavate	*d, ẹing, s*
excavation	*s*
exceed	*ed, ing, ingly, s*
excel	*led, ling, s*
excellent	*ly*
except* (leaving out)	*ed, ing, s*
exception	*al, ally, s*
excess	*ive, ively, es*
exchange	*d, ẹing, able, s*
excitable	
excite	*d, dly, ẹing, ment, s*
exclaim	*ed, ing, s*
exclude	*d, ẹing, s*
exclusive	*ly, ness*
excursion	*s*
excuse	*d, ẹing, s*
execute	*d, ẹing, s*
execution	*er, s*
exercise	*d, ẹing, s*
exert	*ed, ing, ion, s*
exhaust	*ed, ing, ion, ible, ive, -pipe, s*
exhibit	*ed, ing, or, s*
exhibition	*s*
exile	*d, ẹing, s*
exist	*ed, ing, ence, ent, s*
exit	*s*
expand	*ed, ing, s*
expanse	*s*
expansion	*s*

expect	*ed, ing, ant, ation, s*
expedition	*s*
expel	*led, ling, s*
expense	*s*
expensive	*ly, ness*
experience	*d, ẹing, s*
experiment	*ed, ing, al, ally, s*
expert	*ise, ly, ness, s*
expire	*d, ẹing, s*
explain	*ed, ing, s*
explanation	*s*
explode	*d, ẹing, s*
exploit	*s*
exploration	*s*
explore	*d, ẹing, r, s*
explosion	*s*
explosive	*s*
export	*ed, ing, er, s*
expose	*d, ẹing, s*
exposure	*s*
express	*ed, ing, es*
expression	*s*
exquisite	*ly, ness*
extend	*ed, ing, s*
extension	*s*
extensive	*ly, ness*
extent	
exterior	*s*
extinct	*ion*
extinguish	*ed, ing, es*
extra	*s*
extract	*ed, ing, ion, s*
extraordinar *y*	*ily, iness*
extravagance	*s*
extravagant	*ly*
extreme	*ly, s*
extricate	*d, ẹing, s*

ẹ Drop **e** before adding *ing*

* except
accept

ey

eye   *d, ball, brow, lid, sight, sore, s*
eyeing or **eying**
eyelash   *es*

fa

fable   *s*
fabulous   *ly, ness*
face *d, ɇing, -cloth, -flannel, s*
fact   *s*
factor *y*   *ies*
fade   *d, ɇing, s*
faggot   *s*
fail   *ed, ing, ure, s*
faint *er, est, ish, ly, ness, ed, ing, s*
fair* *er, est, ish, ly, ness, ground, s*
fair *y*   *ies*
faith   *s*
faithful   *ly, ness*
fake   *d, ɇing, s*
falcon   *er, s*
fall   *en, ing, s*
false   *hood, r, st, ly, ness*
falter   *ed, ing, s*
fame   *d*
familiar   *ity, ly*
famil *y*   *ies*
famine   *s*
famish   *ed, ing, es*
famous   *ly*
fan *ned, ning, ner, -belt, light, tail, s*
fancy   *ing*
fanc *ied ier, iest, ies, iful, ifully*
fantastic   *ally*
far *ther,* *thest, -away, -off, -fetched*
fare* (price of journey; food) *s*

farewell   *s*
farm *ed, ing, er, -house, yard, s*
fascinate   *d, ɇing, s*
fashion   *able, ably, ed, ing, s*
fast   *er, est, ness, ed, ing, s*
fasten   *ed, ing, er, s*
fat   *ted, ter, test, ness, s*
fatten   *ed, ing, s*
fatt *y*   *ier, iest, iness*
fatal   *ly*
fate* (destiny)   *d, ful, s*
father* (parent)   *less, ly, s*
fathom   *ed, ing, s*
fatigue   *d, ɇing, s*
fault   *ed, ing, less, lessly, s*
fault *y*   *ier, iest, ily, iness*
favour *able, ably, ed, ing, itism, s*
favourite   *s*
fawn   *ed, ing, s*

fe

fear   *ed, ing, some, s*
fearful   *ly, ness*
fearless   *ly, ness*
feast   *ed, ing, s*
feat* (difficult deed)   *s*
feather   *ed, ing, y, -bed, -duster, s*
feature   *d, ɇing, s*
February   *s*
fed
fee   *s*
feeble   *r, st, ness*
feebly
feed   *ing, er, s*
feel   *ing, er, s*
feet* (pl. of foot)

*ɇ Drop **e** before adding* ing

fair	farther	fate	feat
fare	father	fête	feet

*

fi

feign	ed, ing, s
fell	ed, ing, s
fellow	ship, s
felt	
female	s
feminine	s
fence	d, ǿing, r, s
fend	ed, ing, er, s
fern	s
ferocious	ly, ness
ferocity	
ferret	ed, ing, er, s
ferry	-boat, ing, man, men
ferried	ies
fertile	ly
fertilize	d, ǿing, r, s
fester	ed, ing, s
festival	s
festive	ly
festivity	ies
fetch	ed, ing, es
fête* (entertainment; festival)	d, ǿing, s
feud	s
feudal	ism
fever	ish, ishly, s
few	er, est

fi

fiancé* (masc.)	s
fiancée* (fem.)	s
fibre	glass, -tip, s
fiction	al
fictitious	ly, ness
fiddle	d, ǿing, r, stick, s
fidget	ed, ing, y, s
field	ed, ing, sman, smen, er, s

fiend	ish, s
fierce	r, st, ly, ness
fiery	ier, iest, ily, iness
fight	ing, er, s
figure	d, ǿing, s
file	d, ǿing, s
fill	ed, ing, er, s
fillet	ed, ing, s
film	ed, ing, -set, -star, -studio, s
filter	ed, ing, -bed, -paper, -tip, s
filth	
filthy	ier, iest, ily, iness
final	ly, ist, s
finch	es
find* (found)	ing, er, s
fine	d,* ǿing, s
fine	r, st, ly, ness
finger	ed, ing, -mark, -nail, -print, tip, s
finish	ed, ing, es
fiord or **fjord**	s
fir*	-cone, -tree, s
fire	d, ǿing, man, men, place, work, s
fire	-alarm, -brigade, -engine, -escape, s
fire	-drill, -extinguisher, side, -station, s
firm	er, est, ly, ness, s
first	ly, -aid, -class, -floor, hand, -rate, s
fish	ed, ing, -meal, -paste, y, es or **fish**
fisher	man, men, s
fishing	-boat, -line, -net, -rod, -tackle
fishmonger	s
fist	s
fit	ted, ting, ter, test, ful, ly, ness, ment, s
fix	ed, ing, es
fixture	s
fizz	ed, ing, es
fizzy	ier, iest, ily, iness
fizzle	d, ǿing, s

ǿ Drop **e** before adding *ing*

fla   fle   fli   flo   flu   fly

fl				
flag	ged, ging, -day, -pole, -staff, s			
flagon		s		
flake		d, eing, s		
flame	d, eing, -thrower, s			
flamingo		es or s		
flan		s		
flank		ed, ing, s		
flannel		s		
flap	ped, ping, per, jack, s			
flare		d, eing, s		
flash		ed, ing, es		
flash y	ier, iest, ily, iness			
flask		s		
flat	ter, test, ly, ness, let, s			
flatten		ed, ing, s		
flatter	ed, ing, y, er, s			
flavour	ed, ing, less, s			
flaw		ed, less, s		
flea* (insect)	-bite, -bitten, s			
fleck		ed, ing, s		
fledg(e)ling		s		
fled				
flee* (run away)		ing, s		
fleece		d, eing, s		
fleec y	ier, iest, ily, iness			
fleet	ing, er, est, ly, ness, s			
flesh	-coloured, -wound			
flew* (fly)				
flex	ible, ibility, ed, ing, es			
flick		ed, ing, s		
flicker		ed, ing, s		
flier or **flyer**		s		
flight	-deck, -recorder, -test, s			
flims y	ier, iest, ily, iness			
flinch		ed, ing, es		
fling		ing, s		

flint	lock, stone, s
flint y	ier, iest, ily, iness
flip	ped, ping, per, s
flirt	ed, ing, ation, s
flit	ted, ting, s
float	ed, ing, er, s
flock	ed, ing, s
flog	ged, ging, s
flood	ed, ing, gate, lit, -lighting, -light, s
floor	ed, ing, -board, -cloth, -show, s
flop	ped, ping, s
flopp y	ier, iest, ily, iness
floral	ly
florist	s
flounder	ed, ing, s
flour* (ground wheat)	ed, ing, y, s
flourish	ed, ing, es
flow	ed, ing, s
flower*	ed, ing, y, -bed, -garden, -pot, s
flown	
flu* (influenza)	
flue* (chimney-pipe)	-pipe, s
fluent	ly
fluff	ed, ing, s
fluff y	ier, iest, ily, iness
fluid	s
fluke	d, eing, s
flung	
flurry	ing
flurr ied	ies
flush	ed, ing, es
fluster	ed, ing, s
flute	-player, s
flutter	ed, ing, s
fl y	ies
flyer or **flier**	s
flying	-fish, -machine, -saucer, -squad

*e̷ Drop **e** before adding* ing

*	flea	flew
	flee	flue
		flu

flour
flower

fo

fo

foal	ed, ing, s
foam	ed, ing, -rubber, s
foam y	ier, iest, iness
fo'c'sle or **forecastle**	s
focus	ed, ing, es or **foci**
foe	s
fog	ged, ging, -horn, -lamp, -signal, s
fogg y	ier, iest, ily, iness
foil	ed, ing, s
fold	ed, ing, er, s
foliage	
folk	-dance, lore, -song, -tale, s or **folk**
follow	ed, ing, er, s
foll y	ies
fond	er, est, ly, ness
fondle	d, eing, s
food	stuff, store, s
fool	ed, ing, hardy, s
foolish	ly, ness
foot	ing, hold, path, sore, work, **feet**
football	er, s
footprint	s
footstep	s
for*	
forbad or **forbade**	
forbid	den, ding, s
force	d, eing, s
ford	ed, ing, s
fore* (front)	arm, ground, most, man, men
forecast	ing, er, s
forehead	s
foreign	
foreigner	s
forest	ry, er, s
foretell	ing, er, s
foretold	

forever	more
forfeit	ed, ing, ure, s
forgave	
forge	d, eing, r, s
forger y	ies
forget	ting, -me-not, s
forgetful	ly, ness
forgot	ten
forgive	n, eing, ness, s
fork	ed, ing, s
forlorn	ly, ness
form	ed, ing, ation, s
former	ly
formidable	
formula	e or s
fort* (castle)	s
forth* (forward)	coming
fortification	s
fortify	ing
fortif ied	ies
fortnight	ly
fortress	es
fortunate	ly
fortune	-teller, s
forward	ed, ing, ly, ness, s
fossil	s
fought* (fight)	
foul* (dirty)	ed, ing, er, est, ly, ness, s
found	ed, ing, er
foundation	-stone, s
foundr y	ies
fountain	-pen, s
fowl* (bird)	s or **fowl**
fox	es, hounds, hunting, y
foxglove	s
fox-terrier	s
foyer	s

e Drop **e** before adding ing

*	for	fort	forth	foul
	fore	fought	fourth (4th)	fowl
	four (4)			

fr

fu

fr

fraction	s
fracture	d, ėing, s
fragile	ly, ness
fragment	s
fragrance	s
fragrant	ly
frail	er, est, ly, ty, ness
frame	d, ėing, r, work, s
franc* (foreign coin)	s
frank* (candid, etc.)	er, est, ly, ness, s
frankincense	
frantic	ally, ly
fraud	s
fray	ed, ing, s
freak	ish, s
freckle	d, ėing, s
free	d, ing, r, st, ly, dom, -style, way, s
freeze* (ice; cold)	r, s
freezing	-point
freight	er, s
frequent	ly, ed, ing, s
fresh	er, est, ly, ness
freshen	ed, ing, er, s
fret	ted, ting, ful, fully, s
fret	work, saw, s
friar	s
Friday	s
fried	
friend	ship, s
friendly	ier, iest, iness
frieze* (wall decoration)	s
frigate	s
fright	s
frighten	ed, ing, s
frightful	ly, ness
frill	ed, ing, y, s

fringe	d, ėing, s
frisk	ed, ing, s
frisky	ier, iest, ily, iness
fritter	ed, ing, s
frivolous	ly, ness
frizz	ed, ing, es
frizzy	ier, iest, ily, iness
frock	s
frog	-spawn, s
frolic	ked, king, some, s
front	ed, ing, s
frontier	s
frost	ed, ing, -bite, -bitten, s
frosty	ier, iest, ily, iness
froth	ed, ing, s
frothy	ier, iest, ily, iness
frown	ed, ing, s
froze	n
frugal	ity, ly
fruit	-cake, -juice, -tree, s
fry	er, ing
fried	ies

fu

fudge	
fuel	led, ling, s
fugitive	s
fulfil	led, ling, ment, s
full	er, est, y, ness
fumble	d, ėing, r, s
fume	d, ėing, s
fun	fair
funny	ier, iest, ily, iness
function	ed, ing, s
fund	s
funeral	s

ė Drop **e** before adding *ing*

*	franc	freeze
	frank	frieze

ga

fungus	*es* or **fungi**
funnel	*led, ling, s*
fur* (animal's coat)	*rier, s*
furr *y*	*ier, iest, ily, iness*
furious	*ly, ness*
furl	*ed, ing, s*
furnace	*s*
furnish	*ed, ing, ings, es*
furniture	
furrow	*ed, ing, s*
further	*ed, ing, more, most, s*
furthest	
furtive	*ly, ness*
fur *y*	*ies*
furze	*s*
fuse	*d, ∉ing, s*
fuselage	*s*
fuss	*ed, ing, es*
fuss *y*	*ier, iest, ily, iness*
futile	*ly*
future	*s*
fuzz *y*	*ier, iest, ily, iness*

ga

gabardine or **gaberdine**	
gabble	*d, ∉ing, r, s*
gag	*ged, ging, s*
gaiet *y*	*ies*
gaily	
gain	*ed, ing, s*
gait* (way of walking)	*s*
gala	*s*
galactic	
galax *y*	*ies*
gale	*s*
gallant	*ly, s*

galleon	*s*
galler *y*	*ies*
galley	*-slave, s*
gallon	*s*
gallop	*ed, ing, s*
gallows	
gamble* (bet)	*d, ∉ing, r, s*
gambol* (leap; frisk)	*led, ling, s*
game	*r, st, ly, ness, keeper, s*
gander	*s*
gang	*ed, ing, ster, s*
gangway	*s*
gaol or **jail**	*ed, ing, er, s*
gape	*d, ∉ing, r, s*
garage	*d, ∉ing, s*
garbage	
garden	*ed, ing, er, s*
gargle	*d, ∉ing, s*
garland	*ed, ing, s*
garlic	
garment	*s*
garret	*s*
garrison	*ed, ing, s*
garter	*s*
gas	*sed, sing, es*
gash	*ed, ing, es*
gasp	*ed, ing, s*
gate* (door)	*keeper, post, way, s*
gather	*ed, ing, er, s*
gaud *y*	*ier, iest, ily, iness*
gauge	*d, ∉ing, s*
gauntlet	*s*
gauze	*s*
gave	
gay	*er, est*
gaily	
gaze	*d, ∉ing, r, s*

∉ Drop **e** before adding *ing*

*	fur	gait	gamble
	fir	gate	gambol

ge

gear	ed, ing, case, -lever, wheel, s
geese	
Geiger counter	s
gem	s
general	s
generally	
generate	d, ǿing, s
generation	s
generator	s
generosity	
generous	ly
genie	**genii**
genius	es
gentle	r, st, ness, man, men
gently	
genuine	ly, ness
geograph y	ical, ically
geologist	s
geolog y	ical, ically
geometr y	ic, ical, ically
Georgian	s
geranium	s
germ	s
germinate	d, ǿing, s
germination	s
gesticulate	d, ǿing, s
gesture	d, ǿing, s
get	ting, ter, away, s
geyser	s

gh

ghastl y	ier, iest, ily, iness
gherkin	s
ghost	s
ghostl y	ier, iest, ily, iness

gi

giant	-killer, s
gidd y	ier, iest, ily, iness
gift	ed, s
gigantic	ally
giggle	d, ǿing, r, s
gild* (cover with gold)	ed, ing, er, s
gilt* (gold covering)	
ginger	-ale, -beer, bread, -snap, s
gips y or **gyps** y	ies
giraffe	s
girder	s
girl	ish, -friend, s
Girl Guide	s
give	n, ǿing, r, s

gl

glacier	s
glad	der, dest, ly, ness
gladden	ed, ing, s
glade	s
gladiator	s
gladiolus	es or **gladioli**
glamour	
glamorous	ly
glance	d, ǿing, s
glare	d, ǿing, s
glass	es
gleam	ed, ing, s
glean	ed, ing, er, s
glee	ful, fully
glide	d, ǿing, r, s
glimmer	ed, ing, s
glimpse	d, ǿing, s
glint	ed, ing, s
glisten	ed, ing, s

ǿ Drop **e** before adding *ing*

*   gild   gilt
     guild   guilt

gn go   gr_a

glitter	ed, ing, s
gloat	ed, ing, s
globe	-trotter, s
glockenspiel	s
gloom	
gloom y	ier, iest, ily, iness
glor y	ied, ies
glorious	ly
gloss y	ier, iest, ily, iness
glove	-puppet, s
glow	ed, ing, -worm, s
glue	d, ℓing, y, -pot, s
glum	mer, mest, ly, ness

gn

gnash	ed, ing, es
gnat	-bite, s
gnaw	n, ed, ing, er, s
gnome	s

go

goal	keeper, -kick, -mouth, -post, s
goat	herd, skin, s
gobble	d, ℓing, r, s
goblet	s
goblin	s
god	son, father, mother, parent, s
goddess	es
godchild	ren
goes	
going	s
goggle	d, ℓing, s
gold	en, -dust, -field, -mine, -smith
goldfish	es or goldfish
golf	ing, -club, -course, -links, er, s

golliwog	s
gondola	s
gondolier	s
gone	
gong	s
good	-hearted, ly, ness, s
good-bye	s
goose	geese
gooseberr y	ies
gore	d, ℓing, s
gorge	d, ℓing, s
gorgeous	ly, ness
gorilla	s
gorse	s
gosling	s
gossip	ed, ing, er, s
govern	ed, ing, or, ment, s
governess	es
gown	s

gr

grab	bed, bing, ber, s
grace	d, ℓing, s
graceful	ly, ness
gracious	ly, ness
grade	d, ℓing, s
gradient	s
gradual	ly, ness
grain	s
grammar	
gramophone	s
grand	er, est, ly, ness, stand
grand	father, pa, mother, ma, parents
grandad or grand-dad	s
grandchild	ren
grann y	ies

ℓ Drop e before adding ing

grange	s
granite	
grant	ed, ing, s
grape	fruit, -vine, s
graph	ed, ing, s
grapple	d, ǿing, s
grasp	ed, ing, s
grass	ed, ing, es
grass y	ier, iest, iness
grasshopper	s
grass-snake	s
grate* (fireplace; rub)	r,* d, ǿing, s
grateful	ly, ness
grating	s
gratitude	
grave	r, st, ly, ness
grave	-digger, stone, yard, s
gravel	led, ling, ly, -path, pit, s
gravit y	ies
grav y	ies
graze	d, ǿing, s
grease	d, ǿing, r, -paint, -proof, s
greas y	ier, iest, ily, iness
great* (large)	er,* est, ly, ness, s
greed	
greed y	ier, iest, ily, iness
green	er, est, ly, ness, ery, ish, y, s
greengrocer	s
greenhouse	s
greet	ed, ing, s
grenade	s
grenadier	s
grew	
grey	er, est, ly, ness, ish, hound, s
grief	-stricken, s
grievance	s
grieve	d, ǿing, s

grill* (cook)	ed, ing, er, s
grille* (grating)	s
grim	mer, mest, ly, ness
grime	
grim y	ier, iest, ily, iness
grin	ned, ning, ner, s
grind	ing, er, stone, s
grip	ped, ping, per, s
gristle	
grit	ted, ting, ter, s
gritt y	ier, iest, ily, iness
grizzle	d, ǿing, r, s
groan* (moan)	ed, ing, er, s
grocer	s
grocer y	ies
groom	ed, ing, s
groove	d, ǿing, s
grope	d, ǿing, s
grotesque	ly, ness
grotto	es or s
ground	ed, ing, sheet, sman, smen, s
group	ed, ing, -leader, s
grove	s
grovel	led, ling, ler, s
grow	th, ing, er, s
grown* (got bigger)	
grown-up	s
growl	ed, ing, er, s
grub	bed, bing, ber, s
grubb y	ier, iest, ily, iness
grudge	d, ǿing, s
gruel	
gruesome	ly, ness
gruff	er, est, ly, ness
grumble	d, ǿing, r, s
grump y	ier, iest, ily, iness
grunt	ed, ing, er, s

ǿ Drop **e** before adding *ing*

*	grate	grater	grill	groan
	great	greater	grille	grown

gu gy ha

gu

guarantee	d, ing, s
guard	ed, ing, sman, smen, room, s
guardian	s
guess	ed,* ing, es, work
guest* (visitor)	-night, -house, -room, s
guide	d, ǿing, -dog, -book, -post, s
guild* (society)	hall, s
guillotine	d, ǿing, s
guilt* (wrongdoing)	less, lessly
guilt y	ier, iest, ily, iness
guinea-pig	s
guitar	ist, s
gulf	s
gull	s
gull y	ies
gulp	ed, ing, s
gum	med, ming, boil, -tree, s
gumm y	ier, iest, iness
gun	ned, ning, ner, nery, man, men, s
gun	fire, point, powder, shot, smith, s
gurgle	d, ǿing, s
gush	ed, ing, es
gust	ed, ing, s
gust y	ier, iest, ily, iness
gut	ted, ting, s
gutter	s
guy	s
guzzle	d, ǿing, r, s

gy

gymkhana	s
gymnasium	s or **gymnasia**
gymnast	ic, s
gymslip	s
gyps y or **gips** y	ies

ha

habit	s
hack	ed, ing, er, s
haddock	s or **haddock**
hadn't (had not)	
hail	ed, ing, er, stone, storm, s
hair*	dresser, -dryer, pin, -slide, -style, s
hair y	ier, iest, iness
hake	s or **hake**
half	-price, -term, -time, -way, **halves**
halfpenn y	ies or **halfpence**
hall* (room; passage)	way, s
hallo or **hello** or **hullo**	ed, ing, s
halo	es or s
halt	ed, ing, s
halve	d, ǿing, s
hamburger	s
hammer	ed, ing, s
hammock	s
hamper	ed, ing, s
hamster	s
hand	ed, ing, bag, work, writing, ful, s
handcuff	ed, ing, s
handicap	ped, ping, per, s
handicraft	
handiwork	
handkerchief	s
handle	d, ǿing, r, -bar, s
handsome	r, st, ly, ness
hand y	ier, iest, ily, iness
hang	ed, ing, -gliding, -glider, s
hangar* (aeroplane shed)	s
hanger* (for clothes, etc.)	s
happen	ed, ing, s
happ y	ier, iest, ily, iness
harbour	ed, ing, -master, s
hard	er, est, ish, ly, ness, -hearted, ware

ǿ Drop **e** before adding *ing*

*	guessed	guild	guilt	hair	hall	hangar
	guest	gild	gilt	hare	haul	hanger

harden	ed, ing, er, s		**he**	
hardship	s	**head**	ed, ing, ache, long, light, way, s
hare* (animal)	s	**headmaster**	s
hark	en	**headmistress**	es
harm	ed, ing, s	**headquarters**	
harmful	ly, ness	**heal*** (cure)	ed, ing, er, s
harmless	ly, ness	**health**	
harness	ed, ing, es	**health** y	ier, iest, ily, iness
harp	ist, s	**heap**	ed, ing, s
harpoon	ed, ing, -gun, s	**hear*** (listen)	ing, s
harsh	er, est, ly, ness	**heard*** (listened)	
hart* (stag)	s	**heart*** (of body)	ache, -broken, less, s
harvest	ed, ing, er, s	**hearten**	ed, ing, s
hasn't (has not)		**heart** y	ier, iest, ily, iness
haste	d, ∅ing, s	**hearth**	-rug, s
hasten	ed, ing, s	**heat**	ed, edly, ing, er, -stroke, wave, s
hast y	ier, iest, ily, iness	**heath**	land, s
hat	band, -peg, -pin, stand, -trick, ful, s	**heathen**	s
hatch	ed, ing, es	**heather**	s
hatchet	s	**heave**	d, ∅ing, r, s
hate	d, ∅ing, r, s	**heaven**	ly, ward, s
hateful	ly, ness	**heav** y	ier, iest, ily, iness
hatred		**he'd** (he had; he would)	
haught y	ier, iest, ily, iness	**hedge**	d, ∅ing, hog, row, -sparrow, s
haul* (pull)	age, ed, ing, ier, s	**heed**	ed, ing, ful, less, s
haunt	ed, ing, s	**heel*** (back of foot)	ed, ing, s
have	∅ing	**heft** y	ier, iest, ily, iness
haven't (have not)		**helfer**	s
haversack	s	**height**	s
havoc		**heighten**	ed, ing, s
haw	thorn, s	**heir*** (one who inherits)	loom, s
hawk	ed, ing, er, s	**heiress**	es
hay	field, maker, making, rick, stack, s	**held**	
hazard	ed, ing, ous, ously, s	**helicopter**	s
hazel	nut, -tree, s	**he'll** (he will; he shall)	
haze	s	**hello** or **hallo** or **hullo**	ed, ing, s
haz y	ier, iest, ily, iness	**helm**	sman, smen, s

∅ Drop **e** before adding *ing*

hi

ho

helmet	s
help	ed, ing, er, s
helpful	ly, ness
helpless	ly, ness
helter-skelter	s
hem	med, ming, -line, s
her	self, s
herald	ed, ing, s
herb	age, al, alist, s
herd* (of cattle, etc.)	ed, ing, sman, s
here* (in this place)	about(s), by, with
here's (here is)	
hermit	age, -crab, s
hero	es
heroic	al, ally, s
heroine	s
heroism	
heron	s
herring	-gull, s or **herring**
he's (he is; he has)	
hesitate	d, ¢ing, s
hesitation	s
hew* (chop; cut)	n, ed, ing, er, s
hexagon	al, s

hi

hibernate	d, ¢ing, s
hibernation	
hiccup	ed, ing, s
hid	den
hide	¢ing, -and-seek, away, -out, s
hideous	ly, ness
high	er*, est, ly, chair, light, -road, s
highland	er, s
Highness	es
highway	man, men, s

hijack	ed, ing, er, s
hike	d, ¢ing, r, s
hilarious	ly, ness
hill	ock, side, top, s
hill y	ier, iest, iness
him* (he)	self
hinder	ed, ing, s
hindrance	s
hinge	d, ¢ing, s
hint	ed, ing, s
hippopotamus	es or **hippopotami**
hire* (rent)	d, ¢ing, -purchase, r, s
hiss	ed, ing, es
historic	al, ally
histor y	ies
hit	ting, ter, s
hitch	ed, ing, es
hitch-hike	d, ¢ing, r, s
hive	s

ho

hoard* (hidden store)	ed, ing, s
hoarse* (husky)	r, st, ly, ness
hobble	d, ¢ing, s
hobb y	ies
hockey	-stick
hoe	d, ing, s
hog	skin, s
hoist	ed, ing, s
hold	ing, -all, -up, er, s
hole* (hollow place)	d, ¢ing, s
holiday	ed, ing, -camp, -maker, s
hollow	ed, ing, ly, ness, s
holl y	ies
hollyhock	s
holster	s

¢ Drop **e** before adding *ing*

*							
herd	here	hew	higher	him	hoard	hoarse	hole
heard	hear	hue	hire	hymn	horde	horse	whole

hu

hol y* (godly)	ier, iest, ily, iness, ies	hostage	s
home	-grown, -made, work, ward, s	hostel	led, ling, ler, s
homeless	ness	hostess	es
homel y	ier, iest, iness	hostile	ly
homesick	ness	hot	ter, test, ly, ness, house, -plate
honest	ly, y	hotel	ier, s
honey	-bee, dew, -pot, comb, suckle, s	hound	ed, ing, s
honeymoon	ed, ing, er, s	hour* (sixty mins.)	ly, -hand, s
honour	able, ably, ed, ing, s	house	d, ∅ing, hold, work, keeper, s
hood	ed, ing, s	housemaster	s
hoof	beat, mark, s or hooves	housemistress	es
hook	ed, ing, er, s	house wife	wives
hooligan	ism, s	hover	ed, ing, port, s, craft
hoop	ed, ing, -la, s	however	
hoot	ed, ing, er, s	howl	ed, ing, er, s
hop	ped, ping, per, s		
hope	d, ∅ing, s		
hopeful	ly, ness		**hu**
hopeless	ly, ness	huddle	d, ∅ing, s
horde* (crowd)	s	hue* (colour)	s
horizon	tal, tally, s	hug	ged, ging, s
horn	s	huge	r, st, ly, ness
hornpipe	s	hullo or hallo or hello	ed, ing, s
hornet	s	hum	med, ming, mer, s
horoscope	s	human	ity, ly
horrible	ness	humble	d, ∅ing, r, st, ness, s
horribly		humbly	
horrid	ly, ness	humid	ity
horrify	ing	humiliate	d, ∅ing, s
horrif ied	ies	humorous	ly, ness
horror	-stricken, -struck, s	humour	ed, ing, s
horse* (animal)	back, man, men, shoe, s	hump	ed, ing, s
horse-chestnut	-tree, s	hunch	ed, ing, s
hose	d, ∅ing, -pipe, s	hundred	th, weight, s
hospital	s	hung	
hospitality		hunger	ed, ing, s
host	s	hungr y	ier, iest, ily, iness

∅ Drop **e** before adding *ing*

*	holy	horde	horse		hour	hue
	wholly	hoard	hoarse		our	hew

hunt	*ed, ing, sman, smen, er, s*
hurdle	*d, ɇing, r, s*
hurl	*ed, ing, er, s*
hurrah or **hurray**	*ed, ing, s*
hurricane	*-lamp, s*
hurry	*ing*
hurr *ied*	*iedly, ies*
hurt	*ing, s*
hurtle	*d, ɇing, s*
husband	*s*
hush	*ed, ing, es*
husk *y*	*ier, iest, ily, iness*
hustle	*d, ɇing, s*
hutch	*es*

hy

hyacinth	*s*
hydrangea	*s*
hydraulic	*ally, s*
hydrofoil	*s*
hydrogen	
hydroplane	*s*
hyena or **hyaena**	*s*
hygiene	
hygienic	*ally*
hymn* (song of praise)	*al, -book, s*
hypnotism	
hypnotist	*s*
hypnotize	*d, ɇing, s*
hysteric	*al, ally, s*

ic

ice	*d, ɇing, berg, -cream, -cube, s*
icicle	*s*
ic *y*	*ier, iest, ily, iness*

id

I'd (I would; I should; I had)	
idea	*s*
ideal	*ly, ism, ist, s*
identical	*ly*
identification	
identify	*ing*
identif *ied*	*ies*
identit *y*	*ies*
idiot	*s*
idiotic	*al, ally*
idle* (lazy)	*d, ɇing, r, st, ness, s*
idly	
idol* (false god)	*s*
idolize	*d, ɇing, s*

ig

igloo	*s*
ignite	*d, ɇing, s*
ignorance	
ignorant	*ly*
ignore	*d, ɇing, s*

il

I'll (I will)	
ill	*-bred, -mannered, -treated, s*
illness	*es*
illegal	*ly*
illegible	
illiterate	*ly, ness, s*
illuminate	*d, ɇing, s*
illumination	*s*
illusion	*ist, s*
illustrate	*d, ɇing, s*
illustration	*s*

ɇ Drop **e** before adding *ing*

* hymn	idle
him	idol

im

in

im	
I'm (I am)	
image	s
imaginary	
imagination	s
imagine	d, e̸ing, s
imitate	d, e̸ing, s
imitation	s
immediate	ly, ness
immense	ly, ness
immortal	ity, ly, s
immune	
immunize	d, e̸ing, s
impatience	
impatient	ly
imperfect	ion, ly
impersonate	d, e̸ing, s
impersonation	s
impertinence	s
impertinent	ly
implement	s
implore	d, e̸ing, s
impolite	ly, ness
import	ed, ing, er, s
importance	
important	ly
impose	d, ø̸ing, s
impossibility	ies
impossible	
impress	ed, ing, ive, es
impression	able, s
imprison	ed, ing, ment, s
improve	d, e̸ing, ment, s
impudence	
impudent	ly
impure	ly
impurity	ies

in	
inaccurate	ly
inattentive	ly, ness
incapable	
inch	ed, ing, es
incident	al, ally, s
incline	d, e̸ing, s
include	d, e̸ing, s
inclusive	ly, ness
income	s
inconvenience	d, e̸ing, s
inconvenient	ly
incorrect	ly, ness
increase	d, e̸ing, s
incredible	y
incurable	ness, s
indeed	
indefinite	ly, ness
independent	ly
indicate	d, e̸ing, s
indication	s
indicator	s
indigestion	
indignant	ly
indignation	
indistinct	ly, ness
individual	ly, s
indoor	s
industrial	ly
industrious	ly
industry	ies
inexpensive	ly, ness
infant	s
infantry	man, men
infect	ed, ing, ious, ion, s
inferior	ity, ly, s
infirmary	ies

e̸ Drop **e** before adding *ing*

inflammable	*ness*	**inspect**	*ed, ing, ion, or, s*
inflate	*d, ẹing, s*	**inspiration**	*s*
influence	*d, ẹing, s*	**inspire**	*d, ẹing, s*
influenza		**install**	*ed, ing, ation, s*
inform	*ed, ing, ation, er, s*	**instalment**	*s*
infrequent	*ly*	**instance**	*s*
infuriate	*d, ẹing, s*	**instant**	*aneous, ly*
ingredient	*s*	**instead**	
inhabit	*ed, ing, able, ant, s*	**instinct**	*ive, ively, s*
inhale	*d, ẹing, s*	**institute**	*d, ẹing, s*
inherit	*ed, ing, ance, s*	**institution**	*al, s*
initial	*led, ling, s*	**instruct**	*ed, ing, ive, ion, or, s*
inject	*ed, ing, ion, s*	**instrument**	*al, alist, s*
injure	*d, ẹing, s*	**insufficient**	*ly*
injur y	*ies*	**insult**	*ed, ing, s*
ink	*ed, ing, -bottle, -pot, stand, -well, s*	**insurance**	*s*
ink y	*ier, iest, iness*	**insure**	*d, ẹing, s*
inland		**intact**	
inn	*keeper, s*	**intelligence**	
inner	*most*	**intelligent**	*ly*
innings		**intend**	*ed, ing, s*
innocence		**intense**	*ly, ness*
innocent	*ly, s*	**intent**	*ly, ness*
inoculate	*d, ẹing, s*	**intention**	*al, ally, s*
inoculation	*s*	**intercept**	*ed, ing, ive, ion, or s*
inquire or **enquire**	*d, ẹing, r, s*	**interest**	*ed, ing, s*
inquir y or **enquir** y	*ies*	**interfere**	*d, ẹing, nce, s*
inquisitive	*ly, ness*	**interior**	*s*
insane	*ly*	**interlude**	*s*
inscription	*s*	**intermediate**	*ly*
insect	*s*	**international**	*ly*
insensible		**interpret**	*ed, ing, ation, er, s*
insert	*ed, ing, ion, s*	**interrogate**	*d, ẹing, s*
inside	*s*	**interrupt**	*ed, ing, ion, s*
insist	*ed, ing, ence, ent, s*	**interval**	*s*
insolence		**intervene**	*d, ẹing, s*
insolent	*ly*	**interview**	*ed, ing, er, s*

ẹ Drop **e** before adding *ing*

introduce	d, eing, s
introduction	s
intrude	d, eing, r, s
invade	d, eing, r, s
invalid	ed, ing, s
invasion	s
invent	ed, ing, ive, ion, or, s
investigate	d, eing, s
investigation	s
investigator	s
invisible	ness
invitation	s
invite	d, eing, s
involve	d, eing, s
inward	ly, s

ir

iris	es
iron	ed, ing, monger, work, s
ironing-board	s
irregular	ity, ly
irrigate	d, eing, s
irrigation	
irritabl e	y
irritabilit y	ies
irritate	d, eing, s
irritation	s

is

island	er, s
isle* (island)	s
isn't (is not)	
isolate	d, eing, s
isolation	
issue	d, eing, s

it

italic	s
itch	ed, ing, es
itch y	ier, iest, iness
item	s
its* (belonging to it)	
it's* (it is)	
itself	

iv

I've (I have)	
ivor y	ies
iv y	ies

ja

jab	bed, bing, s
jabber	ed, ing, s
jack	ed, ing, pot, s
jackdaw	s
jacket	s
jade	d, eing, s
jagged	ly, ness
jaguar	s
jail or gaol	ed, ing, er, s
jam	med, ming, my, -pot, -jar, s
jamboree	s
jangle	d, eing, s
January	s
jar	red, ring, ful, s
jaunt	ed, ing, s
jaunt y	ier, iest, ily, iness
javelin	s
jaw	-bone, s
jay	s
jazz	ed, ing, y, es

e Drop e before adding ing

* isle / aisle   its / it's

je ji jo ju

je

jealous	ly
jealous y	ies
jeans	
jeep	s
jeer	ed, ing, s
jell y	ied, ies
jelly-fish	es or **jelly-fish**
jemm y	ies
jerk	ed, ing, s
jerk y	ier, iest, ily, iness
jerkin	s
jersey	s
jest	ed, ing, er, s
jet	ted, ting, -liner, -plane, -fighter, s
jettison	ed, ing, s
jett y	ies
Jew*	ish, s
jewel*	led, ling, ler, -case, s
jewellery or **jewelry**	

ji

jiff y	ies
jig	ged, ging, ger, s
jigsaw puzzle	s
jilt	ed, ing, s
jingle	d, ǿing, -jangle, s
jiu-jitsu or **ju-jitsu** or **judo**	
jive	d, ǿing, s

jo

job	less, s
jockey	s
jocular	ity, ly
jodhpurs	

ju

jog	ged, ging, ger, s
join	ed, ing, ery, er, s
joint	ed, ing, ly, s
joist	s
joke	d, ǿing, r, s
jollit y	ies
joll y	ier, iest, ily, iness
jolt	ed, ing, s
jonquil	s
jostle	d, ǿing, s
jot	ted, ting, ter, s
journal	ism, ist, s
journey	ed, ing, s
joust	ed, ing, s
jovial	ity, ly
joy	s
joyful	ly, ness
joyous	ly, ness

ju

jubilant	ly
jubilation	s
jubilee	s
judge	d, ǿing, s
judg(e)ment	s
judo or **ju-jitsu** or **jiu-jitsu**	
juggle	d, ǿing, r, s
juice	s
juic y	ier, iest, ily, iness
July	s
jumble	d, ǿing, -sale, s
jump	ed, ing, er, -jet, s
jumper	s
jump y	ier, iest, ily, iness
junction	s
June	s

ǿ Drop **e** before adding *ing*

*	Jew	jewel
	dew	dual
	due	duel

jungle	s
junior	s
junk	-shop, s
junket	s
juror	s
jur y	ies
just	ly, ness
justice	
justify	ing
justif ied	ies
jut	ted, ting, s
juvenile	s

ka

kaleidoscope	s
kangaroo	s
karate	
kayak	s

ke

keel	ed, ing, s
keen	er, est, ly, ness
keep	ing, er, sake, s
kennel	-maid, s
kept	
kerb* (pavement edge)	side, stone, s
kernel* (nut; seed)	s
kestrel	s
ketchup	
kettle	-holder, ful, s
key*	hole, -ring, s

kh

khaki	s

ki

kick	ed, ing, -off, er, s
kid	skin, s
kidnap	ped, ping, per, s
kidney	-bean, s
kill	ed, ing, er, s
kiln	s
kilogram(me)	s
kilometre	s
kilt	s
kimono	s
kin	sfolk, sman, smen
kind	er, est, -hearted, s
kindl y	ier, iest, ily, iness
kindness	es
kindergarten	s
kindle	d, ҽing, s
king	dom, cup, fisher, s
kink	ed, ing, y, s
kiosk	s
kipper	s
kiss	ed, ing, es
kit	ted, ting, -bag, s
kitchen	ette, -maid, s
kite	s
kitten	s

kn

knack	s
knapsack	s
knave* (rogue)	s
knead* (work dough)	ed, ing, s
knee	-deep, -high, -cap, s
kneel	ed, ing, s
knelt or kneeled	
knew* (know)	

ҽ Drop e before adding ing

*	kerb	kernel	key	knave	knead	knew
	curb	colonel	quay	nave	need	new

la

knife   *d, ∅ing, -edge, -point,* **knives**
knight* (Sir)   *ed, ing, ly, -errant, hood, s*
knit   *ted, ting, ter, s*
knitting-needle   *s*
knob   *s*
knobbl*y*   *ier, iest, iness*
knock   *ed, ing, er, -out, s*
knot* (tied string; sea speed)   *ted, ting, s*
knott*y*   *ier, iest, ily, iness*
know* (understand)   *n, ing, ingly, s*
knowledge   *able*
knuckle   *d, ∅ing, -bone, -duster, s*

la

label   *led, ling, s*
laborator*y*   *ies*
labour   *ed, ing, er, s*
lace   *d, ∅ing, s*
lack   *ed, ing, s*
lacquer   *ed, ing, s*
lacrosse
ladder   *ed, ing, s*
laden
lad*y*   *ies*
ladybird   *s*
lag   *ged, ging, gard, s*
lagoon   *s*
laid
lain* (lie flat)
lair* (den)   *s*
lake   *s*
lamb   *ed, ing, -chop, kin, skin, swool, s*
lame   *d, ∅ing, r, st, ly, ness, s*
lament   *ed, ing, able, ation, s*
lamp   *light, -post, shade, -standard, s*
lance   *d, ∅ing, -corporal, r, s*

land   *ed, ing, mark, scape, slide, slip, s*
landlad*y*   *ies*
landlord   *s*
lane* (narrow road)   *s*
language   *s*
lantern   *s*
lap   *ped, ping, s*
lapel   *s*
lapse   *d, ∅ing, s*
larch   *es*
lard   *ed, ing, s*
larder   *s*
large   *r, st, ly, ness*
lark   *s*
larva* (insect grub)   *e*
lash   *ed, ing, es*
lass   *es*
lasso   *ed, ing, es or s*
last   *ed, ing, ly, s*
latch   *ed, ing, es*
late   *r, st, ly, ness*
lathe   *s*
lather   *ed, ing, s*
latitude   *s*
latter   *ly*
laugh   *able, ed, ing, s*
laughter
launch   *ed, ing, es*
launder   *ette, ed, ing, s*
laundress   *es*
laundr*y*   *ies*
laurel   *s*
lava* (volcanic rock)   *s*
lavator*y*   *ies*
lavender   *-water*
law *ful, less, -breaker, -court, s*
lawyer   *s*

*∅ Drop **e** before adding ing*

	knight	knot	know		lain	lair	larva
*	night	not	no		lane	layer	lava

le   li

lawn   -mower, -sprinkler, s
lay   ing, about, -by, out, er, s
laid
layer* (coat; thickness)   ed, ing, s
laze   d, ∉ing, s
laz y   ier, iest, ily, iness

le

lead* (metal)   ed, en, -poisoning, s
lead (be first)   ing, er, s
leaf   ed, ing, less, -stalk, **leaves**
leaf y   ier, iest, iness
leaflet   s
league   s
leak* (hole; crack)   age, ed, ing, s
leak y   ier, iest, iness
lean   er, est, ly, ness
lean   ed, ing, s
leant* or **leaned**
leap   ed, ing, frog, -year, s
leapt or **leaped**
learn   ed, ing, er, s
learnt or **learned**
least
leather   y, s
leave   ∉ing, r, s
lecture   d, ∉ing, r, s
led* (guided)
ledge   s
leek* (vegetable)   s
left
leg   ged, ging, less, -iron, -rest, s
legend   ary, s
legion   s
leisure   ly
lemon   ade, -drop, -juice, -peel, -tree, s

lend   ing, er, s
length   s
lengthen   ed, ing, s
length y   ier, iest, ily, iness
lenient   ly
lens   es
lent* (lend)
leopard   skin, s
leotard   s
leper   s
leprosy
less   er
lessen* (make smaller)   ed, ing, s
lesson* (thing learnt)   s
let   ting, s
let's (let us)
letter   ed, ing, -writer, s
letter-box   es
lettuce   s
level   led, ling, -crossing, s
lever   age, ed, ing, s

li

liable
liar* (one who lies)   s
liberal   s
libert y   ies
librarian   s
librar y   ies
licence* (noun)   s
license* (verb)   d, ∉ing, s
lick   ed, ing, er, s
licorice or **liquorice**
lie   d, s
lying
lieutenant   -colonel, -general, s

∉ Drop **e** before adding *ing*

*	layer	lead	leak	leant	lessen	liar	licence
	lair	led	leek	lent	lesson	lyre	license

life	*less, like, line, long, size, time.* **lives**	**lo**	
life	*boat, belt, -guard, -jacket, -saving*	**load**	*ed, ing, er, s*
lift	*ed, ing, er, s*	**loaf**	**loaves**
light	*er, est, ly, ness, weight, s*	**loan*** (lend)	*ed, ing, s*
light	*ed, ing, ish, er, house, ship, s*	**loathe**	*d, ǿing, s*
lighten	*ed, ing, s*	**loathsome**	*ly, ness*
lightning	*-conductor*	**lob**	*bed, bing, ber, s*
like	*able, d, ǿing, ness, s*	**lobb**y	*ies*
likely	*ier, iest, ihood*	**lobster**	*-pot, s*
lilac	*-tree, s*	**local**	*ly, s*
lily	*ies*	**localit**y	*ies*
limb	*less, s*	**locate**	*d, ǿing, s*
lime	*-juice, light, -tree, s*	**location**	*s*
limit	*ed, ing, less, s*	**lock**	*ed, ing, er, smith, s*
limp	*ed, ing, er, est, ly, ness, s*	**locket**	*s*
limpet	*s*	**locomotive**	*s*
line	*d, ǿing, sman, smen, s*	**locust**	*s*
linen	*s*	**lodge**	*d, ǿing, r, s*
liner	*s*	**loft**	*s*
linger	*ed, ing, er, s*	**loft**y	*ier, iest, ily, iness*
link	*ed, ing, s*	**log**	*ged, ging, -book, -cabin, s*
linoleum or **lino**	*s*	**loganberr**y	*ies*
lion	*-tamer, s*	**loiter**	*ed, ing, er, s*
lioness	*es*	**loll**	*ed, ing, er, s*
lip	*-reading, stick, s*	**lollipop**	*s*
liquid	*s*	**loll**y	*ies*
liquorice or **licorice**		**lone*** (alone)	*r, some*
list	*ed, ing, s*	**lonel**y	*ier, iest, ily, iness*
listen	*ed, ing, er, s*	**long**	*ed, ing, ingly, er, est, bow, -stop, s*
lit or **lighted**		**longitude**	*s*
literature		**look**	*ed, ing, er, -out, s*
litter	*ed, ing, -basket, -bin, -bug, -lout, s*	**looking-glass**	*es*
little	*ness*	**loom**	*ed, ing, s*
live	*d, ǿing, r, s*	**loop**	*ed, ing, hole, s*
lively	*ier, iest, ily, iness*	**loose**	*r, st, ly, ness*
liver	*ish, s*	**loosen**	*ed, ing, s*
lizard	*s*	**loot*** (plunder)	*ed, ing, er, s*

ǿ Drop **e** before adding *ing*

lu ly ma

lop	*ped, ping, -sided, s*
lord	*ship, s*
lorry	*ies*
lose	*∅ing, r, s*
loss	*es*
lost	
lotion	*s*
lotto	
loud	*er, est, ish, ly, ness, -speaker*
lounge	*d, ∅ing, r, s*
lout	*ish, s*
love	*d, ∅ing, r, bird, -letter, -song, s*
lovely	*ier, iest, ily, iness*
low	*er, est, ly, ness, s*
lower	*ed, ing, s*
lowland	*er, s*
loyal	*ist, ly, ty*
lozenge	*s*

lu

lubricate	*d, ∅ing, s*
lubrication	
luck	*less*
lucky	*ier, iest, ily, iness*
ludo	
lug	*ged, ging, s*
luggage	*-carrier, -rack, -van*
lukewarm	*ly, ness*
lull	*ed, ing, s*
lullaby	*ies*
lumbago	*s*
lumber	*ed, ing, er, jack, -room, s*
luminous	*ly, ness*
lump	*ed, ing, s*
lumpy	*ier, iest, ily, iness*
lunatic	*s*

lunch	*ed, ing, -box, es*
luncheon	*s*
lung	*s*
lunge	*d, ∅ing, s*
lupin	*s*
lurch	*ed, ing, es*
lure	*d, ∅ing, s*
lurk	*ed, ing, er, s*
luscious	*ly, ness*
lustre	*ous*
lusty	*ier, iest, ily, iness*
lute* (musical instrument)	*s*
luxuriant	*ly*
luxurious	*ly, ness*
luxury	*ies*

ly

lying	
lynch	*ed, ing, es*
lynx	*es* or **lynx**
lyre* (musical instrument)	*s*
lyric	*al, s*

ma

macaroni	
mace	*-bearer, s*
machine	*d, ∅ing, -gun, s*
machinery	
machinist	*s*
mackerel	*s* or **mackerel**
mackintosh	*es*
mad	*der, dest, ly, ness, house, man, men*
madden	*ed, ing, s*
madam	*s*
madame (French)	**mesdames**

∅ Drop **e** before adding *ing*

*	lute	lyre
	loot	liar

made* (make)		**maniac**		*s*
magazine	*s*	**manicure**		*d, ℓing, s*
maggot	*y, s*	**manner*** (way; behaviour)		*ed, s*
magic	*al, ally*	**manoeuvre**		*d, ℓing, s*
magician	*s*	**manor*** (lord's land)		*-house, s*
magistrate	*s*	**mansion**		*s*
magnet	*ic, ically, ism, s*	**mantelpiece**		*s*
magnetize	*d, ℓing, s*	**manual**		*ly, s*
magnificent	*ly*	**manufacture**		*d, ℓing, r, s*
magnify	*ing*	**manure**		*d, ℓing, s*
magnif *ied*	*ies*	**manuscript**		*s*
magpie	*s*	**many**		
maid* (girl)	*en, servant, s*	**map** *ped, ping, per, -reading, s*		
mail* (armour; post)	*ed, ing, -bag, s*	**marble**		*s*
maim	*ed, ing, s*	**March**		*es*
main* (chief)	*ly, land, stay, s*	**march**		*ed, ing, es*
maintain	*ed, ing, s*	**mare*** (female horse)		*s*
maison(n)ette	*s*	**margarine**		*s*
maize* (corn)		**margin**		*s*
majest *y*	*ic, ically, ies*	**marigold**		*s*
major	*ette, -general, s*	**marine**		*r, s*
majorit *y*	*ies*	**marionette**		*s*
make *ℓing, -believe, shift, -up, r, s*		**mark** *ed, ing, sman, smen, er, s*		
malaria		**market** *ed, ing, -day, -place, -stall, s*		
male* (man; masculine)	*s*	**marmalade**		*s*
mallet	*s*	**maroon**		*ed, ing, s*
mammal	*s*	**marquee**		*s*
mammoth	*s*	**marriage**		*s*
man *ned, ning, hole, hood,* **men**		**marry**		*ing*
manl *y*	*ier, iest, ily, iness*	**marr** *ied*		*ies*
manage *d, ℓing, able, ably, ment, s*		**marrow**		*s*
manager	*s*	**Mars**		
manageress	*es*	**marsh**		*es*
mandolin	*s*	**marsh** *y*		*ier, iest, iness*
mane* (hair)	*s*	**marshal**		*led, ling, s*
manger	*s*	**marsh-mallow**		*s*
mangle	*d, ℓing, s*	**martyr**		*ed, ing, dom, s*

ℓ Drop **e** before adding *ing*

*	made	mail	main	maize	manner	mare
	maid	male	mane	maze	manor	mayor

me

marvel	*led, ling, s*
marvellous	*ly, ness*
marzipan	
mascot	*s*
masculine	*s*
mash	*ed, ing, es*
mask	*ed, ing, s*
mason	*ry, s*
masquerade	*d, ẹing, r, s*
mass	*ed, ing, es*
massacre	*d, ẹing, s*
massage	*d, ẹing, s*
masseur	*s*
masseuse	*s*
massive	*ly, ness*
mast	*ed, -head, s*
master	*ed, ing, ly, y, mind, piece, s*
mat	*ted, ting, s*
matador	*s*
match	*ed, ing, sticks, wood, box, es*
mate	*d, ẹing, s*
material	*s*
mathematic	*al, ally, ian, s*
matinée	*s*
matron	*s*
matter	*ed, ing, s*
mattress	*es*
maul	*ed, ing, s*
mauve	*r, st, s*
maxim *um*	*a*
may	*be*
May	*s*
maypole	*s*
mayonnaise	
mayor* (head of town or city)	*s*
mayoress	*es*
maze* (puzzle)	*s*

me

meadow	*s*
meagre	*ly, ness*
meal	*-time, s*
mean	*er, est, ly, ness, s*
meaning	*less, s*
meant	
meantime	
meanwhile	
measles	
measure	*d, ẹing, ment, s*
meat* (flesh)	*y, -axe, -ball, -pie, s*
mechanic	*al, ally, s*
mechanism	*s*
mechanize	*d, ẹing, s*
medal* (badge—for bravery, etc.)	*s*
medallion	*s*
meddle* (interfere)	*d, ẹing, some, r, s*
medi(a)eval	
medical	*ly, s*
medicine	*s*
Mediterranean	
medium	*s* or **media**
meek	*er, est, ly, ness*
meet* (come together)	*ing, s*
megaphone	*s*
melod *y*	*ious, iously, ies*
melon	*s*
melt	*ed, ing, s*
member	*ship, s*
memorial	*s*
memorize	*d, ẹing, s*
memor *y*	*ies*
menace	*d, ẹing, s*
menagerie	*s*
mend	*ed, ing, er, s*
mental	*ity, ly*

*ẹ Drop **e** before adding ing*

*	maze	mayor	meat	medal
	maize	mare	meet	meddle

mi

mention	*ed, ing, s*	**might**	
menu	*s*	**might** *y*	*ier, iest, ily, iness*
merchant	*s*	**migrate**	*d, ℓing, s*
merciful	*ly, ness*	**migration**	*s*
merciless	*ly, ness*	**mild**	*er, est, ly, ness*
merc *y*	*ies*	**mildew**	*ed, ℓing, s*
mercury		**mile**	*age, stone, s*
mere	*ly*	**military**	
meringue	*s*	**milk**	*ed, ing, er, man, men, -shake, s*
merit	*ed, ing, s*	**milk** *y*	*ier, iest, ily, iness*
mermaid	*s*	**mill**	*ed, ing, er, -pond, stone, s*
merr *y*	*ier, iest, ily, iment*	**millimetre**	*s*
mesmerize	*d, ℓing, s*	**million**	*th, s*
mess	*ed, ing, es*	**millionaire**	*s*
mess *y*	*ier, iest, ily, iness*	**millionairess**	*es*
message	*s*	**mime**	*d, ℓing, s*
messenger	*s*	**mimic**	*ked, king, s*
metal	*lic, work, -detector, s*	**mince**	*d, ℓing, r, meat, -pie, s*
meteor	*ic, ite, oid, ology, ologist, s*	**mind***	*ed, ing, er, ful, less, -reader, s*
meter* (measuring box)	*s*	**mine**	*d,* ℓing, field, sweeper, s*
method	*ical, ically, s*	**miner*** (mine worker)	*s*
methylated spirit(s)		**mineral**	*s*
metre* (length measure)	*s*	**mingle**	*d, ℓing, s*
mew	*ed, ing, s*	**miniature**	*s*
		minim *um*	*a*
		minister	*s*
mi·		**minnow**	*s*
miaow	*ed, ing, s*	**minor*** (young person; lesser) *s*	
mice		**minstrel**	*s*
microphone	*s*	**mint**	*ed, ing, y, -sauce, s*
microscope	*s*	**minus**	*es*
midday		**minute**	*-hand, s*
middle	*-aged, -class*	**minute** (small)	*ly, ness*
midge	*s*	**miracle**	*s*
midget	*s*	**miraculous**	*ly, ness*
midnight		**mirage**	*s*
midst		**mirror**	*ed, ing, s*
midway			

*ℓ Drop **e** before adding *ing*

mo

mirth	
misbehave	d, ẹing, s
misbehaviour	
mischief	-maker
mischievous	ly, ness
miser	ly, s
miserabl e	y
miser y	ies
misfortune	s
mishap	s
mislay	ing, s
mislaid	
misplace	d, ẹing, s
miss	ed*, ing, es
missile	s
mission	s
missionar y	ies
mist* (haze; fog)	ed, ing, s
mist y	ier, iest, ily, iness
mistake	n, ẹing, s
mistook	
mistletoe	
mistress	es
mistrust	ed, ing, s
mitten	s
mix	ed, ing, es
mixer	s
mixture	s

mo

moan* (groan)	ed, ing, er, s
moat	ed, s
mob	bed, bing, s
mobile	s
moccasin	s
mock	ed, ing, s

mocker y	ies
model	led, ling, ler, s
moderate	d, ẹing, ly, ness, s
modern	ity, ly, ness, s
modernize	d, ẹing, s
modest	ly, y
moist	ure, ly, ness
moisten	ed, ing, s
mole	hill, skin, s
moment	s
monarch	s
monaster y	ies
Monday	s
money	-lender, -order, -spider, s
mongrel	s
monitor	s
monitress	es
monk	s
monkey	-nut, s
monotonous	ly, ness
monster	s
month	s
monthl y	ies
monument	s
mood	s
mood y	ier, iest, ily, iness
moon	beam, less, light, s
moor	hen, land, s
moor	age, ed, ing, s
mop	ped, ping, per, head, s
moral	ly, s
more	over
morning* (a.m.)	s
morsel	s
mortal	ly, s
mortar	-board, s
mosaic	s

ẹ Drop **e** before adding *ing*

*	missed	moan	morning
	mist	mown	mourning

60

mu

mosquito	es
moss	es
moss y	ier, iest, iness
most	ly
motel	s
moth	-eaten, -proof, ball, s
mother	ed, ing, less, ly, hood, s
motion	ed, ing, less, -picture, s
motor	ed, ing, -bike, -boat, -car, ist, s
motor	-cycle, -cyclist, -scooter, way, s
motto	es
mould	ed, ing, er, s
mould y	ier, iest, iness
moult	ed, ing, s
mound	s
mount	ed, ing, s
mountain	ous, side, -top, s
mountaineer	ing, s
mourn ing* (sorrowing)	ed, ful, fully, er, s
mouse	d, ẽing, ẽy, r, -hole, trap. **mice**
moustache	s
mouth	-organ, ful, s
movable	s
move	d, ẽing, r, ment, s
mow	ed, ing, er, s
mown* (cut grass, etc.)	

mu

much	
mud	-bank, -bath, -flat, guard
mudd y	ier, iest, ily, iness
muddle	d, ẽing, r, s
muffle	d, ẽing, r, s
mulberr y	ies
mule	teer, s
multiplication	

my

multiply	ing
multipl ied	ier, ies
multitude	s
mumble	d, ẽing, r, s
mumm y	ies
mumps	
munch	ed, ing, es
mural	s
murder	ed, ing, er, s
murderess	es
murmur	ed, ing, er, s
muscle* (of body)	s
museum	s
mushroom	s
music	al, ally, -case, -hall, -stand
musician	s
musket	eer, -shot, s
mussel* (shellfish)	s
must	
mustn't (must not)	
mustard	-pot
must y	ier, iest, ily, iness
mutineer	s
mutiny	ing
mutin ied	ies
mutter	ed, ing, er, s
mutton	-chop, -cutlet
muzzle	d, ẽing, s

my

myrrh	
myself	
myster y	ies
mysterious	ly, ness
mystify	ing
mystif ied	ies

ẽ Drop **e** before adding ing

*	mourning	mown	muscle
	morning	moan	mussel

na

nail *ed, ing, -scissors, -file, s*
naked *ly, ness*
name *d, ęing, ly, less, -plate, sake, s*
nanny *ies*
napkin *-ring, s*
nappy *ies*
narcissus *es* or **narcissi**
narrate *d, ęing, s*
narrow *ed, ing, er, est, ish, ly, ness, s*
nasturtium *s*
nasty *ier, iest, ily, iness*
nation *al, ally, wide, s*
nationality *ies*
native *s*
nativity *ies*
natural *ly, ness*
naturalist *s*
nature *s*
naughty *ier, iest, ily, iness*
nautical *ly*
naval
nave* (main part of church) *s*
navigate *d, ęing, s*
navigation
navigator *s*
navy *ies*

ne

near *ed, ing, er, est, ly, ness, s*
neat *er, est, ly, ness*
necessary *ily, ies*
necessity *ies*
neck *lace, let, line, tie, s*
need* (want) *ed, ing, s*
needn't (need not)

ni

needle *work, -case, s*
negative *s*
neglect *ed, ing, s*
neglectful *ly, ness*
Negress *es*
Negro *es*
neigh *ed, ing, s*
neighbour *ing, ly, hood, s*
neither
nephew *s*
nerve *d, ęing, -racking, s*
nervous *ly, ness*
nest *ed, ing, -egg, ful, s*
nestle *d, ęing, s*
net *ted, ting, ball, ful, s*
nettle *s*
neutral *s*
never *more, theless*
new* (just made) *er, est, ly, ness*
news *caster, -letter, -reel, -sheet, y*
newsagent *s*
newspaper *man, men, -boy, -girl, s*
newt *s*
next

ni

nibble *d, ęing, r, s*
nice *r, st, ly, ness*
nick *ed, ing, s*
nickname *d, ęing, s*
niece *s*
night* *-club, fall, -light, mare, -time, s*
nightingale *s*
nil
nimble *r, st, ness, -footed*
nimbly

*ę Drop **e** before adding ing*

* nave   need   new   night
   knave   knead   knew   knight

no   nu ny oa

no	
no* (not any; opp. of yes)	es
noble	r, st, man, men, s
nobody	ies
nod	ded, ding, der, s
noise	less, lessly, s
noisy	ier, iest, ily, iness
nomad	ic, s
none* (not any)	
nonsense	
noodle	s
noon	day
noose	s
normal	ly
Norman	s
north	-east, -west, ern, erly, wards
nose	d, ẹing, bag, bleed, dive, gay, s
nostril	s
not* (no)	
notable	s
notch	ed, ing, es
note	d, ẹing, book, case, paper, let, s
nothing	
notice	d, ẹing, able, ably, -board, s
notify	ing
notified	ication, ies
notion	s
nougat	
nought	s
nourish	ment, ed, ing, es
novel	ist, s
novelty	ies
November	s
novice	s
now	adays
nowhere	
nozzle	s

nu	
nuclear	
nude	s
nudist	s
nudge	d, ẹing, s
nugget	s
nuisance	s
numb	ed, ing, ly, ness, s
number	ed, ing, -plate, s
numeral	s
numerical	ly
numerous	ly
nun* (religious woman)	s
nurse	d, ẹing, maid, s
nursery	ies
nut	ted, ting, cracker, shell, -tree, s
nutty	ier, iest, ily, iness
nuthatch	es
nutmeg	s
nutrition	al, ist
nutritious	ly, ness
nuzzle	d, ẹing, s

ny	
nylon	s
nymph	s

oa	
oaf* (stupid person)	ish, s or **oaves**
oak	-apple, -tree, s
oar* (rowing blade)	sman, smen, s
oasis	es
oast	-house, s
oat	meal, cake, s
oath* (promise; swear-word)	s

ẹ Drop **e** before adding *ing*

*	no	none	not		oaf	oar
	know	nun	knot		oath	ore
						or

ob

obedience	
obedient	*ly*
obey	*ed, ing, s*
object	*ed, ing, or, s*
objection	*able, ably, s*
obligation	*s*
oblige	*d, ℓing, s*
obliterate	*d, ℓing, s*
oblong	*s*
oboe	*ℓist, s*
obscure	*d, ℓing, ly, s*
obscurity	
observant	*ly*
observation	*s*
observatory	*ies*
observe	*d, ℓing, r, s*
obstacle	*-course, -race, s*
obstinate	*ly*
obstruct	*ed, ing, ion, s*
obtain	*able, ed, ing, s*
obvious	*ly, ness*

oc

occasion	*al, ally, s*
occupant	*s*
occupation	*s*
occupy	*ing*
occupied	*ier, ies*
occur	*red, ring, rence, s*
ocean	*s*
o'clock	
octagon	*al, s*
October	*s*
octopus	*es* or **octopodes**
oculist	*s*

od

odd	*er, est, ly, ness, ment, s*
odious	*ly, ness*
odour	*s*

of

of	
off	*ing, hand, chance, -side, spring*
offence	*s*
offend	*ed, ing, er, s*
offensive	*ly, ness*
offer	*ed, ing, s*
offertory	*ies*
office	*-block, -boy, -girl, -worker, s*
officer	*s*
official	*ly, s*
often	*er, est*

og

ogre	*s*
ogress	*es*

oi

oil	*ed, ing, can, -rig, -stove, -well, s*
oil	*-heater, -painting, skin, -tanker, s*
oily	*ier, iest, ily, iness*
ointment	*s*

ol

old	*en, er, est, ish, -time*
old-fashioned	*ness*
olive	*-oil, -grove, -tree, s*
Olympic Games or **Olympics**	

*ℓ Drop **e** before adding ing*

om on op   or os ot

om

omelet(te)	s
omen	s
omission	s
omit	ted, ting, s
omnibus	es

on

once	
oncoming	
one*	self, -sided, s
onion	y, -skin, s
onlooker	s
only	
onslaught	s
onto	
onward	s

op

opal	s
opaque	ly, ness
open	ed, ing, ly, ness, er, s
opera	-glasses, -house, -singer, s
operatic	s
operate	d, ǿing, s
operation	s
operator	s
opinion	s
opponent	s
opportunity	ies
oppose	d, ǿing, s
opposite	ly, ness
opposition	
optician	s
optimist	ic, ically, s

or

oral	ly
orange	ade, -blossom, -peel, -tree, s
orang-(o)utan	s
orator	s
orbit	ed, ing, s
orchard	s
orchestra	l, s
orchid	s
ordeal	s
order	ed, ing, s
orderly	iness, ies
ordinary	ily, iness
ore* (metal in rock)	s
organ	-grinder, -loft, -pipe, ist, s
organization	s
organize	d, ǿing, r, s
orient	
oriental	s
origin	s
original	ity, ly
originate	d, ǿing, s
ornament	ed, ing, al, ation, s
ornithologist	s
ornithology	
orphan	ed, ing, age, s

os

osier	s
ostrich	es

ot

other	s
otherwise	
otter	s

ǿ Drop **e** before adding *ing*

*	one (1)	ore
	won	oar
		or

ou ov   ow ox oy

ou

ought	
ounce	s
our* (belonging to us)	s
ourselves	
out	come, let, look, put, right, standing
outbreak	s
outburst	s
outcast	s
outer	most
outfit	ted, ting, ter, s
outhouse	s
outing	s
outlaw	ed, ing, s
outline	d, éing, s
outnumber	ed, ing, s
out-patient	s
outpost	s
outrage	d, éing, s
outrageous	ly, ness
outside	r, s
outskirts	
outward	ly, ness, s
outwit	ted, ting, s

ov

oval	s
oven	s
over	s
overall	s
overbalance	d, éing, s
overboard	
overcame	
overcome	éing, s
overcoat	s
overcrowd	ed, ing, s

overdose	d, éing, s
overflow	ed, ing, s
overhaul	ed, ing, s
overhead	s
overhear	ing, s
overheard	
overjoyed	
overlap	ped, ping, s
overload	ed, ing, s
overlook	ed, ing, s
overpower	ed, ing, s
overseas	
oversleep	ing, s
overslept	
overtake	n, éing, s
overtook	
overthrow	n, ing, s
overthrew	
overtime	
overturn	ed, ing, s
overwhelm	ed, ing, s
overwork	ed, ing, s

ow

owe	d, éing, s
owl	et, s
own	ed, ing, er, s

ox

ox	en
oxlip	s
oxygen	

oy

oyster	-bed, -catcher, -farm, -shell, s

é Drop e before adding ing.

* our / hour

pa

pa	
pace	d, ∅ing, r, s
Pacific	
pack	ed, ing, er, s
package	d, ∅ing, s
packet	ed, ing, s
pad	ded, ding, der, s
paddle	d, ∅ing, r, -boat, -steamer, s
padlock	ed, ing, s
page	-boy, s
pageant	s
paid	
pail* (bucket)	ful, s
pain* (suffering)	ed, ing, -killer, s
painful	ly, ness
painless	ly, ness
paint	ed, ing, er, s
pair* (two)	ed, ing, s
palace	s
pale* (faint; whitish)	r, st, ly, ness, s
palette	s
palm	-tree, s
pamper	ed, ing, er, s
pamphlet	s
pan	ned, ning, ful, cake, s
panda	s
pane* (sheet of glass)	s
panel	led, ling, list, s
panic	ked, king, ky, -stricken, -struck, s
panorama	s
pans y	ies
pant	ed, ing, s
panther	s
pantomime	s
pantr y	ies
paper	ed, ing, -boy, -girl, -chain, -clip, s
papier mâché	

parachute	d, ∅ing, -troops, s
parade	d, ∅ing, -ground, s
paraffin	-heater, -oil
parallel	ed, ing, s
paralyse	d, ∅ing, s
paralys is	es
paratroops	
parcel	led, ling, s
parch	ed, ing, es
parchment	s
pardon	able, ed, ing, s
pare* (cut away; peel)	d, ∅ing, s
parent	age, al, s
parish	es
park	ed, ing, land, -keeper, s
parliament	s
parrot	s
parsley	-sauce
parsnip	s
parson	age, s
part	ed, ing, ly, s
particle	s
particular	ly, s
partition	ed, ing, s
partner	ed, ing, ship, s
partridge	s
part y	ies
pass	ed*, ing, able, es
passage	way, s
passenger	s
passion	ate, ately, s
passport	s
password	s
past* (time gone by)	
paste	d, ∅ing, s
pastel* (crayon)	led, ling, s
pastille* (sweet)	s

∅ Drop **e** before adding *ing*

*	pail	pain	pair	passed	pastel
	pale	pane	pare	past	pastille
			pear		

pe

pastime	s
pastry	ies
pasture	d, ℯing, s
pasty	ies
pat	ted, ting, s
patch	ed, ing, work, es
patchy	ier, iest, ily, iness
path	way, s
pathetic	ally
patience	
patient	ly, s
patrol	led, ling, man, men, -leader, s
patter	· ed, ing, s
pattern	ed, ing, -book, s
pause* (hesitate)	d, ℯing, s
pave	d, ℯing, ment, s
pavilion	s
paw (animal's foot)	s,* ed, ing
pawn	ed, ing, broker, shop, -ticket, s
pay	able, ing, er, ment, -day, -desk, s
paid	

pe

pea	nut, -pod, -soup, -shooter, s
peace* (quiet)	able, -offering, -time
peaceful	ly, ness
peach	es
peacock	s
peahen	s
peak	ed, ing, s
peal* (sound of bells)	ed, ing, s
pear* (fruit)	-drop, -tree, s
pearl	-diver, -fisher, s
peasant	ry, s
peat	-bog, -moor, y
pebble	-stone, s
pebbly	ier, iest, iness

peck	ed, ing, er, s
peculiar	ly
peculiarity	ies
pedal* (foot-lever)	led, ling, -cycle, s
peddle* (to hawk goods)	d, ℯing, s
pedestrian	s
pedigree	s
pedlar	s
peel* (skin of fruit)	ed, ing, er, s
peep	ed, ing, er, -hole, -show, s
peer* (stare)	ed, ing, s
peg	ged, ging, s
Pekin(g)ese	**Pekin(g)ese**
pelican	s
pellet	s
pelt	ed, ing, s
pen	ned, ning, -friend, -nib, s
penalty	ies
pence	
pencil	led, ling, -case, -sharpener, s
pendulum	s
penetrate	d, ℯing, s
penguin	s
peninsula	n
pen knife	knives
pennant	s
penny	ies or **pence**
penniless	ly, ness
pension	ed, ing, able, er, -book, s
people	s
pepper	ed, ing, y, -pot, mint, s
perambulator	s
perch	ed, ing, es
percussion	-band, s
perfect	ly, ed, ing, ion, s
perform	ed, ing, ance, er, s
perfume	d, ℯing, s

ℯ Drop **e** before adding *ing*

* pause	peace	pear	peal	pedal	peer
paws	piece	pair	peel	peddle	pier
		pare			

ph

perhaps	
peril	*ous, ously, s*
period	*ic, ical, ically, s*
periscope	*s*
perish	*ed, ing, es*
permanent	*ly*
permission	
permit	*ted, ting, s*
perplex	*ed, ing, es*
persevere	*d, ɇing, ɇance, s*
persist	*ed, ing, ence, ent, s*
person	*al, ally, s*
perspiration	
perspire	*d, ɇing, s*
persuade	*d, ɇing, s*
persuasion	
persuasive	*ly, ness*
pessimist	*ic, ically, s*
pester	*ed, ing, s*
pet	*ted, ting, -shop, s*
petal	*s*
petrol	*eum, -pump, -station, s*
petticoat	*s*
pew	*s*
pewter	

ph

phantom	*s*
pheasant	*s*
philatelist	*s*
phone	*d, ɇing, -booth, s*
photo	*-fit, -frame, s*
photograph	*ed, ing, y, er, s*
physical	*ly*
physician	*s*
physics	

pi

pi

pi* ($\pi = 3.14159$)	
pianist	*s*
piano	*-accordian, -stool, s*
piccolo	*-player, s*
pick	*ed, ing, er, axe, pocket, s*
pickle	*d, ɇing, r, s*
picnic	*ked, king, ker, -basket, s*
picture	*d, ɇing, -book, -frame, s*
picturesque	*ly, ness*
pie*	*crust, -shop, s*
piece* (a part)	*d, ɇing, s*
pier* (jetty)	*s*
pierce	*d, ɇing, s*
pierrot	*s*
pig	*let, skin, s*
pigst *y*	*ies*
pigeon	*-hole, -house, -loft, s*
pigm *y* or pygm *y*	*ies*
pigtail	*s*
pike	*man, men, staff, s*
pilchard	*s*
pile	*d, ɇing, s*
pilgrim	*age, s*
pillar	*s*
pillar-box	*es*
pillion	*-rider, -seat, s*
pillow	*case, slip, -fight, s*
pilot	*ed, ing, s*
pimple	*d, ɇing, s*
pimpl *y*	*ier, iest, iness*
pin	*ned, ning, cushion, s*
pincers	**pincers**
pinch	*ed, ing, es*
pine	*d, ɇing, apple, -cone, -needle, -tree, s*
pink	*er, est, ish, y, ness, s*
pint	*s*

ɇ Drop **e** before adding *ing*

pl   po

pioneer	ed, ing, s
pipe	d, ǿing, r, -cleaner, ful, s
piranha	s
pirate	s
pistil* (part of flower)	s
pistol* (small gun)	-shot, s
pit	ted, ting, fall, -head, -prop, s
pitch	ed, ing, -black, -dark, es
pitchfork	ed, ing, s
piteous	ly
pity	ing
pitied	iful, iless, ies
pixie	s or **pix**y, ies
pizza	s

pl

placard	s
place* (position)	d, ing, s
plague	d, ǿing, s
plaice* (fish)	**plaice**
plain*	er, est, ly, ness, s
plait	ed, ing, s
plan	ned, ning, ner, s
plane* (tool; to smooth)	d, ǿing, s
plane* (aeroplane; tree)	s
planet	s
plank	ed, ing, s
plant	ed, ing, ation, er, s
plaster	ed, ing, er, s
plastic	s
plasticine	
plate	d, ǿing, ful, -glass, -rack, s
platform	s
platinum	
play	ed, ing, ground, mate, time, er, s
play	-group, -pen, thing, wright, s
playful	ly, ness

plead	ed, ing, s
pleasant	ly, ness
please	d, ǿing, s
pleasure	s
pleat	ed, ing, s
plentiful	ly, ness
plenty	
pliers	**pliers**
plimsoll	s
plod	ded, ding, der, s
plot	ted, ting, ter, s
plough	ed, ing, man, men, boy, s
pluck	ed, ing, er, s
plucky	ier, iest, ily, iness
plug	ged, ging, ger, s
plum*	-pudding, -stone, -tree, s
plumage	
plumb*	ed, ing, -line, s
plumber	s
plump	er, est, ly, ness
plunder	ed, ing, er, s
plunge	d, ǿing, r, s
plural	s
plus	es

po

poach	ed, ing, es
poacher	s
pocket	ed, ing, -book, -money, ful, s
pocket-knife	-knives
podgy	ier, iest, ily, iness
poem	s
poet	ic, ical, ically, s
poetry	
point	ed, ing, -blank, -duty, less, er,'s
poise	d, ǿing, s
poison	ed, ing, ous, ously, er, s

ǿ Drop **e** before adding *ing*

*	pistil	place	plain	plum
	pistol	plaice	plane	plumb

poke	*d, ǿing, r, s*	**portable**	*s*
polar bear	*s*	**porter**	*s*
pole* (long rod)	*-jump, -vault, s*	**porthole**	*s*
police	*d, ǿing, -officer, man, woman*	**portion**	*ed, ing, s*
police force	*s*	**portrait**	*s*
police station	*s*	**pose**	*d, ǿing, s*
polish	*ed, ing, es*	**position**	*ed, ing, s*
polite	*r, st, ly, ness*	**positive**	*ly, ness*
political	*ly*	**possess**	*ed, ing, ive, es*
politician	*s*	**possession**	*s*
poll* (vote)	*ed, ing, s*	**possibilit** *y*	*ies*
pollen		**possible**	*s*
polo	*-stick*	**possibly**	
polytechnic	*s*	**post**	*ed, ing, man, men, card, mark, s*
polythene		**postage**	*-stamp*
pomp	*ous, ously, osity*	**postal order**	*s*
pond	*-life, -snail, weed, s*	**poster**	*s*
ponder	*ed, ing, s*	**post office**	*s*
pontoon	*-bridge, s*	**postpone**	*d, ǿing, ment, s*
pon *y*	*ies*	**pos** *y*	*ies*
poodle	*s*	**pot**	*ted, ting, ful, -luck, -hole, -shot, s*
pool	*ed, ing, s*	**potato**	*es*
poor* (not rich)	*er, est, ly, ness*	**potion**	*s*
pop	*ped, ping, per, corn, gun, s*	**potter**	*ed, ing, s*
pop	*-group, -music, -singer, -song, s*	**potter** *y*	*ies*
poplar	*-tree, s*	**pouch**	*es*
popp *y*	*ies*	**poultice**	*d, ǿing, s*
popular	*ity, ly*	**poultry**	*-farm*
population		**pounce**	*d, ǿing, s*
porcelain		**pound**	*ed, ing, s*
porch	*es*	**pour*** (flow out)	*ed, ing, er, s*
porcupine	*s*	**pout**	*ed, ing, er, s*
pore* (study; tiny hole)	*d, ǿing, s*	**poverty**	*-stricken*
pork	*-butcher, -chop, -pie, er, y*	**powder**	*ed, ing, y, -puff, -room, s*
porpoise	*s*	**power**	*ed, -house, -plant, -station, s*
porridge		**powerful**	*ly, ness*
port	*s*	**powerless**	*ly, ness*

ǿ Drop **e** before adding *ing*

*	pole	poor
	poll	pore
		pour

pr_a pre   pri   pro

pr

practical	*ly, ity, ness*
practice* (noun)	*s*
practise* (verb)	*d, ǝing, s*
prairie	*s*
praise	*d, ǝing, s*
prance	*d, ǝing, s*
prank	*ster, s*
prawn	*ed, ing, er, s*
pray* (ask God)	*ed, ing, s*
prayer	*-book, -meeting, s*
preach	*ed, ing, es*
preacher	*s*
precaution	*ary, s*
precious	*ly, ness*
precipice	*s*
prefect	*s*
prefer	*red, ring, able, ably, ence, s*
prehistoric	*al, ally*
preliminar*y*	*ies*
premises	
preparation	*s*
prepare	*d, ǝing, s*
prescribe	*d, ǝing, s*
prescription	*s*
presence	
present	*ed, ing, ation, s*
presently	
preserve	*d, ǝing, s*
president	*s*
press	*ed, ing, es*
pressure	*-cooker, -gauge, s*
pretend	*ed, ing, er, s*
prett*y*	*ier, iest, ily, iness*
prevent	*ed, ing, ion, s*
previous	*ly, ness*
prey* (victim; thing hunted)	*ed, ing, s*

price	*d, ǝing, less, -list, -tag, s*
prick	*ed, ing, er, s*
prickle	*d, ǝing, s*
prickl*y*	*ier, iest, iness*
pride* (proudness)	*d, ǝing, s*
pried* (looked into)	
priest	*ly, hood, s*
priestess	*es*
primary school	*s*
primitive	*ly, ness*
primrose	*s*
prince	*ly, s*
princess	*es*
principal* (head; chief)	*ly, s*
principle* (rule; truth)	*s*
print	*ed, ing, er, s*
prison	*er, s*
private	*ly, s*
privilege	*d, ǝing, s*
prize	*d, ǝing, -winner, s*
probabilit*y*	*ies*
probable	*s*
probably	
problem	*s*
procedure	*s*
proceed	*ed, ing, s*
process	*ed, ing, es*
procession	*s*
proclaim	*ed, ing, s*
procure	*d, ǝing, s*
prod	*ded, ding, s*
produce	*d, ǝing, r, s*
product	*ive, ion, s*
profession	*al, ally, s*
professor	*s*
profit* (gain)	*able, ed, ing, eer, s*
programme	*d, ǝing, r, s*

*ǝ Drop **e** before adding ing*

*	practice	pray	pride	principal	profit
	practise	prey	pried	principle	prophet

progress	*ed, ing, es*
prohibit	*ed, ing, s*
project	*ed, ing, ile, ion, or, s*
promenade	*d, ǿing, r, s*
prominent	*ly*
promise	*d, ǿing, s*
promote	*d, ǿing, r, s*
promotion	*s*
prompt	*ed, ing, er, est, ly, ness, s*
pronounce	*d, ǿing, ment, s*
proof	*s*
prop	*ped, ping, s*
propel	*led, ling, ler, s*
proper	*ly*
propert y	*ies*
prophec y (noun)	*ies*
prophes y (verb)	*ied, ies*
prophesying	
prophet* (foreteller of future)	*s*
proposal	*s*
propose	*d, ǿing, r, s*
proprietor	*s*
prosecute	*d, ǿing, s*
prosper	*ed, ing, ous, ously, ity, s*
protect	*ed, ing, ion, ive, or, s*
protest	*ed, ing, s*
Protestant	*s*
protrude	*d, ǿing, s*
proud	*er, est, ly*
prove	*d, ǿing, s*
proverb	*s*
provide	*d, ǿing, r, s*
provision	*ed, ing, s*
prowl	*ed, ing, er, s*
prune	*d, ǿing, s*
pry	*ing*
pr ied*	*ies*

pu

public	*ly, -house*
publication	*s*
publicity	
publish	*ed, ing, es*
publisher	*s*
pudding	*s*
puddle	*s*
puff	*ed, ing, er, s*
puff y	*ier, iest, ily, iness*
pull	*ed, ing, er, s*
pullover	*s*
pulley	*-block, s*
pulp	*ed, ing, er, s*
pulpit	*s*
pulse	*d, ǿing, s*
pump	*ed, ing, s*
pumpkin	*s*
punch	*ed, ing, es*
punctual	*ity, ly*
puncture	*d, ǿing, s*
punish	*able, ed, ing, es*
punishment	*s*
punt	*ed, ing, er, s*
pupa	*e*
pupil	*s*
puppet	*ry, -play, -show, s*
pupp y	*ies*
purchase	*d, ǿing, r, s*
pure	*r, st, ly, ness*
purity	
purple	*r, st, ness, s*
purpose	*ly, s*
purr	*ed, ing, s*
purse	*r, -snatcher, s*
pursue	*d, ǿing, r, s*
pursuit	*s*

ǿ Drop **e** before adding *ing*

*	prophet	pried
	profit	pride

push	ed, ing, es
puss y	ies
put	ting, s
putt (golf)	ed, ing, er, s
putting-green	s
putty	
puzzle	d, ẽing, r, ment, s

py

pygm y or **pigm** y	ies
pyjamas	
pylon	s
pyramid	s
python	s

qua

quack	ed, ing, s
quadrangle	s
quadruplet	s
quaint	er, est, ly, ness
quake	d, ẽing, s
qualification	s
qualify	ing
qualif ied	ies
qualit y	ies
quantit y	ies
quarantine	d, ẽing, s
quarrel	led, ling, ler, some, s
quarry	ing
quarr ied	ies
quart (two pints)	s*
quarter	ed, ing, s
quartet(te)	s
quartz* (rock-crystal)	
quay* (wharf)	side, s

que

queen	s
queer	er, est, ly, ness
quell	ed, ing, s
quench	ed, ing, es
query	ing
quer ied	ies
quest	ed, ing, s
question	ed, ing, er, -master, s
queue* (line of persons, etc.)	d, r, s
queueing or **queuing**	

qui

quibble	d, ẽing, r, s
quick	er, est, ly, ness
quicken	ed, ing, s
quiet	ed, ing, er, est, ly, ness, s
quieten	ed, ing, s
quill	s
quilt	ed, ing, s
quince	s
quinine	
quintet(te)	s
quintuplet	s
quire* (measure of paper)	s
quit	ted, ting, ter, s
quite	
quiver	ed, ing, s
quiz	zed, zing, zes

quo

quoit	s
quota	s
quotation	-mark, s
quote	d, ẽing, s

ẽ Drop **e** before adding ing

*	quarts	quay	queue	quire
	quartz	key	cue	choir

ra

re_a

ra

rabbit	*ed, ing, er, -hole, -warren, s*
race	*d, ȩing, r, course, horse, track, s*
rack	*ed, ing, s*
racket* (noise)	*ed, ing, eer, s*
racket* or **racquet*** (bat)	*s*
radar	
radiate	*d, ȩing, s*
radiator	*s*
radio	*ed, ing, s*
radish	*es*
radi *us*	*i*
raffle	*d, ȩing, r, -ticket, s*
raft	*s*
rafter	*s*
rag	*ged, ging, s*
ragged	*ly, ness*
rage	*d, ȩing, s*
raid	*ed, ing, er, s*
rail	*ing, s*
railway	*-carriage, -crossing, -line, s*
rain*	*ed, ing, -water, bow, coat, drop, s*
rain *y*	*ier, iest, ily, iness*
raise* (lift up)	*d, ȩing, s*
raisin	*s*
rake	*d, ȩing, r, s*
rally	*ing*
rall *ied*	*ies*
ram	*med, ming, rod, s*
ramble	*d, ȩing, r, s*
ramshackle	
ranch	*es*
rancher	*s*
random	*ly*
rang	
range	*d, ȩing, r, s*
rank	*ed, ing, s*

re

ransack	*ed, ing, er, s*
ransom	*ed, ing, s*
rap* (knock)	*ped, ping, s*
rapid	*ity, ly, s*
rare	*r, st, ly, ness*
rascal	*ly, s*
rash	*er, est, ly, ness*
rasher	*s*
raspberr *y*	*ies*
rat	*ted, ting, -hole, -poison, -trap, s*
rate	*d, ȩing, payer, s*
rather	
ration	*ed, ing, s*
rattle	*d, ȩing, r, snake, s*
rave	*d, ȩing, s*
raven	*s*
ravenous	*ly, ness*
ravine	*s*
raw	*er, est, ly, ness*
ray (beam of light)	*s**
razor	*-blade, -edge, -shell, s*

re

reach	*ed, ing, es*
react	*ed, ing, ion, or, s*
read*	*ing, er, s*
read *y*	*ier, iest, ily, iness*
real* (true)	*ly, ist, istic, ism*
realit *y*	*ies*
realize	*d, ȩing, s*
really	
reap	*ed, ing, er, s*
reappear	*ed, ing, ance, s*
rear	*ed, ing, guard, -lamp, -light, ward, s*
rearrange	*d, ȩing, ment, s*
reason	*ed, ing, able, ably, s*

ȩ Drop **e** before adding *ing*

*	racket	rain	raise	rap	read	read	real
	racquet	reign	rays	wrap	reed	red	reel
		rein					

rebel *led, ling, s*	**refer** *red, ring, s*
rebellion *s*	**referee** *d, ing, s*
rebellious *ly, ness*	**reference** *-book, s*
rebound *ed, ing, s*	**reflect** *ed, ing, ion, or, s*
recall *ed, ing, s*	**refrain** *ed, ing, s*
recapture *d, ẹing, s*	**refresh** *ed, ing, es*
receipt *ed, ing, -book, s*	**refreshment** *s*
receive *d, ẹing, r, s*	**refrigerator** *s*
recent *ly, ness*	**refuge** *s*
receptacle *s*	**refugee** *s*
reception *ist, s*	**refund** *ed, ing, s*
recess *ed, ing, es*	**refusal** *s*
recipe *s*	**refuse** *d, ẹing, s*
recital *s*	**regain** *ed, ing, s*
recitation *s*	**regard** *ed, ing, less, lessly, s*
recite *d, ẹing, s*	**regatta** *s*
reckless *ly, ness*	**regiment** *ed, ing, al, s*
reckon *ed, ing, er, s*	**region** *al, s*
recognize *d, ẹing, s*	**register** *ed, ing, s*
recollect *ed, ing, ion, s*	**regret** *ted, ting, table, tably, s*
recommend *ed, ing, ation, s*	**regretful** *ly*
record *ed, ing, -player, s*	**regular** *ity, ly*
recorder *s*	**regulate** *d, ẹing, s*
recover *ed, ing, s*	**regulation** *s*
recovery *ies*	**rehearsal** *s*
recreation *-ground, s*	**rehearse** *d, ẹing, s*
recruit *ed, ing, ment, s*	**reign*** (rule) *ed, ing, s*
rectangle *s*	**rein*** (strap) *ed, ing, s*
red* (colour) *der, dest, dish, dy, ness, s*	**reindeer** **reindeer**
redden *ed, ing, s*	**reinforce** *d, ẹing, ment, s*
redskin *s*	**reject** *ed, ing, ion, s*
redecorate *d, ẹing, s*	**rejoice** *d, ẹing, s*
reduce *d, ẹing, s*	**rejoin** *ed, ing, s*
reduction *s*	**relate** *d, ẹing, s*
reed* (tall grass) *s*	**relation** *s*
reef *-knot, s*	**relative** *s*
reel* (spool; dance; stagger) *ed, ing, s*	**relax** *ed, ing, es*

*ẹ Drop **e** before adding ing*

*	red	reed	reel	reign
	read	read	real	rein
				rain

rem	ren	rep	req	res	ret	rev	rew

relay	*ed, ing, -race, s*		**request**	*ed, ing, s*
release	*d, ẹing, s*		**require**	*d, ẹing, ment, s*
reliable	*ness*		**rescue**	*d, ẹing, r, s*
relic	*s*		**resemblance**	*s*
relief			**resemble**	*d, ẹing, s*
relieve	*d, ẹing, s*		**reservation**	*s*
religion	*s*		**reserve**	*d, ẹing, s*
religious	*ly, ness*		**reservoir**	*s*
rely	*ing*		**reside**	*d, ẹing, nce, nt, s*
rel*ied*	*iable, ies*		**resign**	*ed, ing, ation, s*
remain	*ed, ing, der, s*		**resist**	*ed, ing, ance, s*
remark	*ed, ing, able, ably, s*		**resolution**	*s*
remed*y*	*ies*		**resort**	*ed, ing, s*
remember	*ed, ing, s*		**respect**	*ed, ing, able, ably, ful, fully, s*
remembrance	*s*		**responsibilit***y*	*ies*
remind	*ed, ing, er, s*		**responsible**	
remnant	*s*		**rest**	*ed, ing, -cure, -home, -room, s*
remote	*ly, ness*		**restful**	*ly, ness*
removal	*s*		**restless**	*ly, ness*
remove	*d, ẹing, r, s*		**restaurant**	*s*
renew	*ed, ing, able, al, s*		**result**	*ed, ing, s*
rent	*ed, ing, able, al, s*		**resume**	*d, ẹing, s*
repair	*ed, ing, able, er, s*		**retire**	*d, ẹing, ment, s*
repay	*ing, able, ment, s*		**retrace**	*d, ẹing, s*
repaid			**retreat**	*ed, ing, s*
repeat	*ed, edly, ing, er, s*		**retrieve**	*d, ẹing, r, s*
repetition	*s*		**return**	*ed, ing, able, -ticket, s*
replace	*d, ẹing, able, ment, s*		**reveal**	*ed, ing, s*
replay	*ed, ing, s*		**revenge**	*d, ẹing, s*
reply	*ing*		**reverse**	*d, ẹing, s*
repl*ied*	*ies*		**review**	*ed, ing, s*
report	*ed, ing, er, s*		**revive**	*d, ẹing, s*
represent	*ed, ing, ative, s*		**revolt**	*ed, ing, s*
reproduce	*d, ẹing, s*		**revolution**	*s*
reptile	*s*		**revolve**	*d, ẹing, s*
republic	*an, s*		**revolver**	*s*
reputation	*s*		**reward**	*ed, ing, s*

ẹ Drop **e** before adding *ing*

rh

rheumatism	
rhinoceros	es
rhododendron	s
rhubarb	
rhyme	d, éing, s
rhythm	ic, ical, ically, s

ri

rib	bed, bing, s
ribbon	s
rice	-pudding, -field, s
rich	er, est, ly, ness, es
rick	ed, ing, s
ricket y	iness
ridden	
riddle	d, éing, r, s
ride	éing, r, s
riding	-crop, -school, -stable, -whip, s
ridge	s
ridicule	d, éing, s
ridiculous	ly, ness
rifle	d, éing, man, men, -range, -shot, s
rig	ged, ging, ger, s
right* (true; opp. left)	ful, ly, -handed, s
rigid	ity, ly, ness
rim	med, ming, less, s
rind	s
ring* (circle)	ed, ing, leader, -master, s
ring* (bell sound)	ing, er, s
rink	s
rinse	d, éing, r, s
riot	ed, ing, er, s
rip	ped, ping, per, -cord, s
ripe	r, st, ly, ness
ripen	ed, ing, s

ripple	d, éing, s
rise	éing, r, s
risen	
risk	ed, ing, s
risk y	ier, iest, ily, iness
rissole	s
rival	led, ling, s
rivalr y	ies
river	-bank, -bed, -boat, side, s
rivet	ed, ing, er, s

ro

road* (highway)	side, way, -sweeper, s
roam	ed, ing, er, s
roar	ed, ing, er, s
roast	ed, ing, er, s
rob	bed, bing, ber, s
robber y	ies
robe	d, éing, s
robin	-redbreast, s
robot	s
rock	ed, ing, -cake, -garden, s
rock y	ier, iest, ily, iness
rocker y	ies
rocket	ed, ing, s
rode* (ride)	
rodeo	s
roe* (deer; fish eggs)	s
rogue	s
rôle* (actor's part)	s
roll* (turn over)	ed, ing, -call, mop, er, s
roller-skate	d, éing, r, s
Roman	s
romance	d, éing, s
romantic	ally, s
romp	ed, ing, er, s

é Drop **e** before adding *ing*

*	right	ring	road	roe	rôle
	write	wring	rode	row	roll
			rowed		

ru

sa

roof	-garden, -rack, -top, s
rook	s
rooker y	ies
room	ful, s
room y	ier, iest, ily, iness
root* (part of a plant)	ed, ing, s
rope	d, ǿing, -ladder, s
rose	-bud, -garden, -hip, -tree, wood, s
rosette	s
ros y	ier, iest, ily, iness
rot	ted, ting, s
rotate	d, ǿing, s
rotten	ly, ness
rough	ed, ing, er, est, ly, ness, s
roughen	ed, ing, s
round	ed, ing, ish, ness, sman, smen, s
roundabout	s
rounders	
rouse	d, ǿing, s
route* (a way)	d, ǿing, s
routine	s
rove	d, ǿing, r, s
row (quarrel)	ed, ing, s
row* (line; use oars)	ed,* ing, er, -boat, s
rowing-boat	s
rowd y	ier, iest, ily, iness, ies
royal	ist, ly, ty

ru

rub	bed, bing, s
rubber	-stamp, -tree, s
rubbish	-tip, -heap, y
rubble	
rub y	ies
rucksack	s
rudder	s

rude	r, st, ly, ness
ruffian	s
ruffle	d, ǿing, s
Rugby	-ball
rugged	ly, ness
ruin	ed, ing, ous, s
rule	d, ǿing, r, s
rumble	d, ǿing, s
rummage	d, ǿing, -sale, s
rumour	ed, ing, s
run	ning, ner, way, s
rung* (ring; ladder step)	s
rural	ly, ness
rush	ed, ing, es
rust	ed, ing, less, -proof, s
rust y	ier, iest, ily, iness
rustle	d, ǿing, r, s
rut	ted, ting, s
rutt y	ier, iest, iness

sa

sabbath	s
sack	ed, ing, ful, -race, s
sacred	ly, ness
sacrifice	d, ǿing, s
sad	der, dest, ly, ness
sadden	ed, ing, s
saddle	d, ǿing, r, -bag, s
safari	s
safe	r, st, ly, ness, s
safety	-catch, -lamp, -net, -pin, -valve
sag	ged, ging, s
sago	s
said	
sail* (travel by ship)	ed, ing, s
sailor	s

ǿ Drop **e** before adding *ing*

*	root	row	rowed	rung	sail
	route	roe	road	wrung	sale
			rode		

SC

saint	s
saintl y	ier, iest, ily, iness
sake	s
salad	-dressing, -oil, s
salar y	ies
sale* (selling)	sman, smen, -room, s
salmon	**salmon**
saloon	s
salt	ed, ing, -water, -cellar, -spoon, s
salt y	ier, iest, iness
salute	d, ɇing, s
salvage	d, ɇing, s
same	ness
sample	d, ɇing, r, s
sanatorium	s or **sanatoria**
sanctuar y	ies
sand	-castle, -dune, paper, -storm, s
sand y	ier, iest, iness
sandal	s
sandwich	ed, ing, es
sang	
sank	
Santa Claus	
sap	ped, ping, ling, s
sapphire	s
sarcastic	ally
sardine	s
sash	es
satchel	s
satellite	s
satin	s
satisfaction	
satisfactor y	ily, iness
satisfy	ing
satisf ied	ies
saturate	d, ɇing, s
Saturday	s

sauce	pan, s
saucer	ful, s
sauc y	ier, iest, ily, iness
saunter	ed, ing, s
sausage	-meat, -roll, s
savage	d, ɇing, ly, ry, ness, s
save	d, ɇing, s
saviour	s
saw	ed, ing, dust, mill, s
sawn or **sawed**	
Saxon	s
saxophone	s
say	ing, s
said	

SC

scabbard	s
scaffold	ing, s
scald	ed, ing, s
scale	d, ɇing, s
scalp	ed, ing, s
scamp	ed, ing, s
scamper	ed, ing, s
scan	ned, ning, ner, s
scar	red, ring, s
scarce	r, st, ly, ness
scarcit y	ies
scare	d, ɇing, r, crow, s
scarf	-ring, s or **scarves**
scarlet	s
scatter	ed, ing, -brain, s
scavenge	d, ɇing, r, s
scene* (view; place)	-shifter, s
scenery	
scent* (smell; perfume)	ed, ing, s
scheme	d, ɇing, r, s

ɇ Drop **e** before adding *ing*

*	sale	scene scent
	sail	seen sent

se

scholar	ship, s
scholastic	ally
school	ed, ing, boy, girl, -teacher, s
schoolmaster	s
schoolmistress	es
schooner	s
science	-fiction, s
scientific	ally
scientist	s
scissors	**scissors**
scold	ed, ing, er, s
scone	s
scoop	ed, ing, er, s
scooter	s
scorch	ed, ing, es
score	d, ∉ing, r, -board, -card, s
scorn	ed, ing, er, s
scornful	ly, ness
scorpion	s
scoundrel	s
scour	ed, ing, er, s
scout	ed, ing, er, master, s
scowl	ed, ing, er, s
scragg y	ier, iest, ily, iness
scramble	d, ∉ing, r, s
scrap	ped, ping, py, -book, -heap, s
scrape	d, ∉ing, r, s
scratch	ed, ing, es
scratch y	ier, iest, ily, iness
scrawl	ed, ing, er, s
scrawl y	ier, iest, iness
scream	ed, ing, er, s
screech	ed, ing, es
screech y	ier, iest, ily, iness
screen	ed, ing, s
screw	ed, ing, driver, s
scribble	d, ∉ing, r, s

scripture	s
scroll	s
scrub	bed, bing, ber, s
scrum	med, ming, mage, s
scuffle	d, ∉ing, r, s
scull* (oar; to row)	ed, ing, er, s
sculler y	ies
sculptor	s
sculptress	es
sculpture	d, ∉ing, s
scuttle	d, ∉ing, s
scythe	d, ∉ing, s

se

sea*	side, sick, shore, front, port, s
sea*	-gull, -horse, -lion, -serpent, s
sea*	man, men, -shell, -water, weed, s
Sea Scout	s
seal	ed, ing, er, skin, s
sealing* (fastening)	-wax
seam* (join; rock vein)	less, s
search	ed, ing, es
searchlight	s
season	-ticket, s
seat	ed, ing, er, -belt, s
seclude	d, ∉ing, s
second	ly, -class, -hand, -rate, s
secondary	
secrecy	
secret	ive, ly, s
secretar y	ies
section	s
secure	d, ∉ing, ly, ness, s
securit y	ies
see* (notice)	ing, s
seed	ed, ing, y, ling, -bed, -cake, s

∉ Drop **e** before adding ing

*	scull	sea	sealing	seam
	skull	see	ceiling	seem

seek	ing, er, s		serpent	s
seem* (appear)	ed, ing, s		servant	-girl, s
seen* (noticed)			serve	d, ǿing, r, s
see-saw	ed, ing, s		service	d, ǿing, s
seize	d, ǿing, s		serviette	s
seldom			session	s
select	ed, ing, ion, s		set	ting, ter, -square, s
self	-conscious, -service, **selves**		settee	s
selfish	ly, ness		settle	d, ǿing, r, ment, s
sell* (exchange for money)	ing, er,* s		several	
sellotape	d, ǿing, s		severe	r, st, ly
semicircle	s		severity	
semicircular	ly		sew* (stitch)	ed, ing, er, s
semi-detached			sewing-machine	s
semolina			sewn* (fastened with stitches)	
send	ing, er, s		sextet(te)	s
senior	s			
sensation	al, ally, s			
sense	d, ǿing, s		**sh**	
senseless	ly, ness		shabb y	ier, iest, ily, iness
sensible	ness		shack	s
sensibly			shade	d, ǿing, s
sent* (send)			shad y	ier, iest, ily, iness
sentence	d, ǿing, s		shadow	ed, ing, s
sentinel	s		shadow y	ily, iness
sentr y	ies		shaft	s
separate	d, ǿing, ly, ness, s		shagg y	ier, iest, ily, iness
separation	s		shake	n, ǿing, r, s
September	s		shak y	ier, iest, ily, iness
sequin	s		shall	
serenade	d, ǿing, r, s		shallow	er, est, ly, ness, s
serf* (villein; slave)	dom, s		shamble	d, ǿing, s
sergeant	-major, s		shame	d, ǿing, s
serial* (in parts—as story or film)	s		shameful	ly, ness
series			shameless	ly, ness
serious	ly, ness		shampoo	ed, ing, s
sermon	s		shamrock	s

ǿ Drop **e** before adding *ing*

shand *y* *ies*	**shingle** *s*
shan't (shall not)	**ship** *ped, ping, load, mate, yard, s*
shant *y* *ies*	**shipwreck** *ed, ing, s*
shape *d, ǿing, ly, s*	**shirk** *ed, ing, er, s*
shapeless *ly, ness*	**shirt** *-button, -sleeve, -tail, s*
share *d, ǿing, s*	**shiver** *ed, ing, y, s*
shark *skin, s*	**shoal** *ed, ing, s*
sharp *er, est, ly, ness, -shooter, s*	**shock** *ed, ing, s*
sharpen *ed, ing, er, s*	**shodd** *y* *ier, iest, ily, iness*
shatter *ed, ing, s*	**shoe*** *ing, -bag, horn, -lace, maker, s*
shave *n, d, ǿing, r, s*	**shod**
shawl *s*	**shone**
sheaf **sheaves**	**shoo*** (frighten away) *ed, ing, s*
shear* (cut; clip) *ed, ing, er, s*	**shook**
sheath *s*	**shoot*** (fire) *ing, er, s*
sheath*-knife* *-knives*	**shop** *ped, ping, per, keeper, lifter, s*
shed *ding, der, s*	**shore*** (sea shore) *s*
sheep *-dog, -farmer, -pen, skin,* **sheep**	**shorn**
sheer* (steep)	**short** *age, er, est, ly, ness, bread, s*
sheet *s*	**shorten** *ed, ing, s*
sheik(h) *s*	**shorthand**
shelf **shelves**	**shot** *-gun, s*
shell *ed, ing, er, s*	**should**
shellfish *es or* **shellfish**	**shouldn't** (should not)
she'll (she will; she shall)	**shoulder** *ed, ing, -bag, -blade, -strap, s*
shelter *ed, ing, s*	**shout** *ed, ing, er, s*
shepherd *s*	**shovel** *led, ling, ler, ful, s*
shepherdess *es*	**show** *n, ed, ing, -case, room, s*
sherbet *s*	**show** *-jumping, -ground, s*
sheriff *s*	**shower** *ed, ing, -bath, s*
sherr *y* *ies*	**shower** *y* *ier, iest, iness*
she's (she is; she has)	**shrank**
shield *ed, ing, s*	**shred** *ded, ding, der, s*
shift *ed, ing, y, er, s*	**shrewd** *er, est, ly, ness*
shin *ned, ning, -guard, -pad, s*	**shriek** *ed, ing, er, s*
shine *ǿing, s*	**shrill** *ed, ing, er, est, y, ness, s*
shin *y* *ier, iest, ily, iness*	**shrimp** *ed, ing, er, s or* **shrimp**

ǿ Drop **e** before adding *ing*

shrine	s
shrink	ing, able, age, s
shrivel	led, ling, s
shrub	s
shrubber y	ies
shrug	ged, ging, s
shrunk	en
shudder	ed, ing, s
shuffle	d, ɇing, r, s
shun	ned, ning, s
shunt	ed, ing, er, s
shut	ting, s
shutter	ed, ing, s
shuttle	d, ɇing, cock, s
shy	er, est, ly, ness

si

sick	er, est, ly, ness, -bay, -bed, -room
sicken	ed, ing, s
side	d, ɇing, car, light, line, -show, s
sideboard	s
sideways	
siege	s
sieve	d, ɇing, s
sift	ed, ing, er, s
sigh	ed, ing, s
sight* (see)	ed, ing, less, seeing, seer, s
sign	ed, ing, board, -writer, post, s
signal	led, ling, ler, man, men, s
signal-box	es
signature	-tune, s
signet* (a seal)	-ring, s
significance	
significant	ly
signify	ing
signif ied	ies

silence	d, ɇing, r, s
silent	ly
silhouette	d, ɇing, s
silk	en, worm, s
silk y	ier, iest, ily, iness
sill y	ier, iest, ily, iness, ies
silver	ed, ing, y, -paper, -plated
similar	ly
similarit y	ies
simmer	ed, ing, s
simple	r, st, ness, ton, -minded
simplicity	
simply	
simplify	ing
simplif ied	ication, ies
simultaneous	ly, ness
sin	ned, ning, ner, s
since	
sincere	r, st, ly, ness
sincerity	
sing	ing, er, -song, s
singe	d, ing, s
single	d, ɇing, ɇy, -handed, s
singular	ly, s
sinister	ly
sink	ing, er, s
sip	ped, ping, per, s
siphon	ed, ing, s
sister	ly, s
sister(s)-**in-law**	
sit	ting, ter, s
sitting-room	s
site* (a place)	d, ɇing, s
situated	
situation	s
size	d, ɇing, s
sizzle	d, ɇing, s

ɇ Drop **e** before adding *ing*

*	sight	signet
	site	cygnet

sk sl

sk

skate	d, ȩing, r, board, s
skating-rink	s
skein	s
skeleton	s
sketch	ed, ing, es
sketch y	ier, iest, ily, iness
skewer	ed, ing, s
ski	-ed, -ing, er, -jump, -lift, -run, s
skid	ded, ding, s
skilful	ly, ness
skill	ed, s
skim	med, ming, mer, s
skin	ned, ning, -diving, -diver, s
skinn y	ier, iest, iness
skip	ped, ping, per, s
skipping-rope	s
skipper	ed, ing, s
skirmish	ed, ing, es
skirt	ed, ing, s
skittle	d, ȩing, r, -alley, -ball, -pin, s
skull* (head bones)	-cap, s
skulk	ed, ing, s
skunk	s
sky	ing, lark, light, -rocket, scraper
sk ied	ies

sl

slack	ed, ing, er, est, ly, ness, s
slacken	ed, ing, s
slain	
slam	med, ming, s
slang	ing, y
slant	ed, ing, wise, s
slap	ped, ping, per, dash, stick, s
slash	ed, ing, es

slate	s
slaughter	ed, ing, er, -house, s
slave	d, ȩing, r, ry, -driver, -trader, s
slay* (kill)	ing, er, s
sledge	d, ȩing, r, s
sleek	ed, ing, er, est, ly, ness, s
sleep	ing, er, less, -walking, -walker, s
sleep y	ier, iest, ily, iness
slept	
sleet	ed, ing, s
sleet y	ier, iest, iness
sleeve	d, less, -button, s
sleigh* (sledge)	ing, -bell, -horse, s
slender	ly, ness
sleuth	-hound, s
slew	
slice	d, ȩing, r, s
slick	ed, ing, er, est, ly, ness, s
slid	
slide	ȩing, r, s
slight	ed, ing, er, est, ly, ness, s
slim	med, ming, mer, mest, ly, ness, s
slime	
slim y	ier, iest, ily, iness
sling	ing, er, s
slink	ing, er, s
slink y	ier, iest, ily, iness
slip	ped, ping, knot, shod, way, s
slipper	s
slipper y	ier, iest, ily, iness
slit	ting, ter, s
slither	ed, ing, y, s
sloe* (wild plum)	-tree, s
slog	ged, ging, ger, s
slogan	s
slop	ped, ping, -basin, s
slopp y	ier, iest, ily, iness

ȩ Drop **e** before adding *ing*

*	skull	slay	sloe
	scull	sleigh	slow

sm

slope	d, ∉ing, s
slot	ted, ting, -machine, -meter, s
slouch	ed, ing, es
slovenly	ier, iest, iness
slow*	ed, ing, er, est, ly, ness, s
slow-worm	s
slug	s
sluggish	ly, ness
sluice	d, ∉ing, -gate, s
slum	my, -dweller, s
slumber	ed, ing, er, s
slump	ed, ing, s
slung	
slunk	
slush	ed, ing, es
slushy	ier, iest, ily, iness
sly	er, est, ly, ness

sm

smack	ed, ing, s
small	er, est, ness
smart	ed, ing, er, est, ly, ness, s
smarten	ed, ing, s
smash	ed, ing, es
smear	ed, ing, s
smeary	ier, iest, ily, iness
smell	ed, ing, er, s
smelly	ier, iest, ily, iness
smelt or **smelled**	
smile	d, ∉ing, r, s
smirk	ed, ing, er, s
smithereens	
smock	ed, ing, s
smoke	d, ∉ing, r, -bomb, -screen, s
smoky	ier, iest, ily, iness
smooth	ed, ing, er, est, ly, ness, s

sn

smother	ed, ing, s
smoulder	ed, ing, s
smudge	d, ∉ing, s
smudgy	ier, iest, ily, iness
smuggle	d, ∉ing, r, s
smut	ted, ting, s
smutty	ier, iest, ily, iness

sn

snack	-bar, s
snail	s
snake	d, ∉ing, ∉y, -bite, -charmer, s
snap	ped, ping, per, shot, dragon, s
snare	d, ∉ing, r, s
snarl	ed, ing, er, s
snatch	ed, ing, es
sneak	ed, ing, er, s
sneaky	ier, iest, ily, iness
sneer	ed, ing, er, s
sneeze	d, ∉ing, r, s
sniff	ed, ing, er, s
sniffle	d, ∉ing, r, s
snigger	ed, ing, er, s
snip	ped, ping, per, s
snipe	d, ∉ing, r, s
snivel	led, ling, ler, s
snob	bery, bish, bishness, s
snooker	ed
snore	d, ∉ing, r, s
snort	ed, ing, er, s
snow	ed, ing, drift, fall, flake, storm, s
snow	man, men, -plough, drop, shoe, s
snowball	ed, ing, s
snowy	ier, iest, ily, iness
snug	ger, gest, ly, ness
snuggle	d, ∉ing, s

∉ Drop **e** before adding *ing*

* slow
  sloe

so   spₐ

so				
soak	ed, ing, s		**soon**	er, est
soap	ed, ing, -suds, -bubble, -flake, s		**soot**	
soapy	ier, iest, ily, iness		**soot**y	ier, iest, ily, iness
soar* (fly upwards)	ed, ing, s		**soothe**	d, ǿing, s
sob	bed, bing, s		**soprano**	s
sociable	ness		**sore*** (painful)	r, st, ly, ness, s
social	ly, s		**sorrow**	ed, ing, ful, fully, s
socialist	s		**sorr**y	ier, iest, ily, iness
society	ies		**sort**	ed, ing, er, s
sock	s		**soul*** (spirit)	ful, fully, s
socket	s		**sound**	ed, ing, er, est, ly, ness, s
soda -bread, -fountain, -water			**soup**	-plate, -spoon, s
sodden			**sour**	ed, ing, er, est, ly, ness, s
sofa	s		**source**	s
soft	er, est, ish, ly, ness, -hearted		**south**	-east, -west, ern, erly, ward
soften	ed, ing, er, s		**souvenir**	s
soggy	ier, iest, ily, iness		**sovereign**	s
soil	ed, ing, s		**sow*** (scatter seed)	ed, ing, er, s
sold* (sell)			**sown*** (planted)	
solder	ed, ing, s			
soldier	ed, ing, s		**sp**	
sole* (only)	ly		**space**	d, ǿing, r, s, craft, man, men
sole* (bottom-of shoe, etc.)	d,* ǿing, s		**space**	-capsule, ship, -station, suit, s
sole* (fish)	s or **sole**		**spacious**	ly, ness
solemn	ity, ly, ness		**spade**	ful, s
solicitor	s		**spaghetti**	
solid	ity, ly, s		**span**	ned, ning, s
solitary			**spangle**	d, ǿing, s
solo	ist, -singer, s		**spaniel**	s
solution	s		**spank**	ed, ing, s
solve	d, ǿing, s		**spanner**	s
some* body, one, how, thing, where			**spare**	d, ǿing, s
sometime	s		**spark**	ed, ing, s
somersault	ed, ing, s		**sparkle**	d, ǿing, r, s
son* (boy)	ny, s		**sparrow**	-hawk, s
song ster, -book, -bird, -writer, s			**spastic**	s

ǿ Drop **e** before adding *ing*

*	soar	sold	sole	some	son	sow	sown
	sore	soled	soul	sum	sun	sew	sewn
						so	

spe   sph   spi   spl   spo   spr   spu   spy

spat	
spawn	*ed, ing, s*
speak	*ing, er, s*
spear	*ed, ing, man, men, head, -gun, s*
special	*ly, ty, ist, ity*
specialize	*d, ę̃ing, s*
specimen	*s*
speck	*ed, ing, less, lessly, s*
speckle	*d, ę̃ing, s*
spectacle	*s*
spectacular	*ly*
spectator	*s*
spectre	*s*
sped or **speeded**	
speech	*-training, less, es*
speed	*ed, ing, -boat, -limit, way, s*
speed *y*	*ier, iest, ily, iness*
spell	*ed, ing, er, bind, bound, s*
spelt or **spelled**	
spend	*ing, er, thrift, s*
spent	
sphere	*s*
spider	*y, s*
spied	
spike	*d, ę̃ing, s*
spill	*ed, ing, s*
spilt or **spilled**	
spin	*ning, ner, -dryer, s*
spinach	
spinster	*s*
spiral	*led, ling, ly, s*
spire	*s*
spirit	*ed, ing, -level, -lamp, s*
spirt or **spurt**	*ed, ing, s*
spit	*ting, ter, s*
spite	*d, ę̃ing, s*
spiteful	*ly, ness*

splash	*ed, ing, es*
splendid	*ly*
splendour	*s*
splint	*s*
splinter	*ed, ing, y, s*
split	*ting, ter, s*
splutter	*ed, ing, er, s*
spoil	*ed, ing, er, -sport, s*
spoilt or **spoiled**	
spoke (speak)	*n, sman, smen*
spoke (of wheel)	*s*
sponge	*d, ę̃ing, r, -bag, -cake, s*
spong *y*	*ier, iest, ily, iness*
spool	*s*
spoon	*ed, ing, ful, s*
sport	*ed, ing, sman, smen, s*
sport *y*	*ier, iest, ily, iness*
spot	*ted, ting, ter, less, lessly, light, s*
spott *y*	*ier, iest, ily, iness*
spout	*ed, ing, s*
sprain	*ed, ing, s*
sprang	
sprat	*s* or **sprat**
sprawl	*ed, ing, er, s*
spray	*ed, ing, er, s*
spread	*ing, er, s*
spring	*ing, -cleaning, -board, time, s*
spring *y*	*ier, iest, ily, iness*
sprinkle	*d, ę̃ing, r, s*
sprint	*ed, ing, er, s*
sprout	*ed, ing, s*
sprung	
spun	
spur	*red, ring, s*
spurt or **spirt**	*ed, ing, s*
spy	*ing*
sp *ied*	*ies*

ę̃ Drop **e** before adding *ing*

sq st_a

sq

squabble	*d, ∉ing, r, s*
squad	*ron, s*
squall	*ed, ing, y, s*
squander	*ed, ing, er, s*
square	*d, ∉ing, ly, ness, -dance, root, s*
squash	*ed, ing, y, es*
squat	*ted, ting, ter, s*
squaw	*s*
squawk	*ed, ing, er, s*
squeak	*ed, ing, er, s*
squeak *y*	*ier, iest, ily, iness*
squeal	*ed, ing, er, s*
squeeze	*d, ∉ing, r, s*
squelch	*ed, ing, es*
squib	*s*
squint	*ed, ing, er, s*
squire	*d, ∉ing, s*
squirm	*ed, ing, er, s*
squirrel	*s*
squirt	*ed, ing, er, s*

st

stab	*bed, bing, ber, s*
stable	*d, ∉ing, -man, -men, -boy, s*
stack	*ed, ing, s*
stadium	*s* or **stadia**
staff	*ed, ing, -room, s*
stag	*-beetle, -horn, hound, -hunt, s*
stage	*d, ∉ing, -hand, -manager, s*
stage-coach	*es*
stagger	*ed, ing, er, s*
stain	*ed, ing, less, er, s*
stair*	*-carpet, case, -rod, way, s*
stake* (a stick; bet)	*d, ∉ing, s*
stale	*r, st, ly, ness*

stalk	*ed, ing, er, s*
stall	*ed, ing, -holder, s*
stallion	*s*
stammer	*ed, ing, er, s*
stamp	*ed, ing, -album, -collector, s*
stampede	*d, ∉ing, s*
stand	*ing, s*
standard	*-bearer, s*
star	*red, ring, less, light, lit, s*
starr *y*	*ier, iest, ily, iness*
starboard	
starfish	*es* or **starfish**
starch	*ed, ing, es*
stare* (look at)	*d, ∉ing, s*
starling	*s*
start	*ed, ing, er, s*
startle	*d, ∉ing, s*
starvation	
starve	*d, ∉ing, s*
state	*d, ∉ing, ment, s*
statel *y*	*ier, iest, ily, iness*
station	*ed, ing, -master, s*
stationary* (still)	
stationer	*s*
stationery* (paper, pens, etc.)	
statue	*tte, s*
staunch	*ed, ing, er, est, ly, ness, es*
stay	*ed, ing, er, s*
steady	*ing*
stead *ied*	*ier, iest, ily, iness, ies*
steak* (meat)	*s*
steal* (thieve)	*ing, s*
stealth	
stealth *y*	*ier, iest, ily, iness*
steam	*ed, ing, er, boat, ship, -engine, s*
steam *y*	*ier, iest, ily, iness*
steel* (metal)	*ed, ing, y, work, worker, s*

∉ Drop **e** before adding *ing*

*	stair	stake		stationary	steal
	stare	steak		stationery	steel

steep	er, est, ly, ness	**stool**	-ball, s
steeple	chase, jack, s	**stoop**	ed, ing, s
steer	age, ed, ing, er, sman, smen, s	**stop**	ped, ping, page, per, s
steering-wheel	s	**storage**	
stem	med, ming, s	**store**	d, ✗ing, house, keeper, -room, s
stencil	led, ling, ler, s	**storey*** (floor)	s
step	ped, ping, -ladder, s	**stork**	s
step	father, mother, brother, sister, s	**storm**	ed, ing, -cloud, s
stepping-stone	s	**storm** y	ier, iest, ily, iness
sterilize	d, ✗ing, r, s	**stor** y* (tale; floor)	ies
stern	er, est, ly, ness	**stout**	er, est, ly, ness, ish, hearted
stew	ed, ing, er, -pot, s	**stove**	-pipe, s
steward	s	**stow**	ed, ing, away, s
stewardess	es	**straggle**	d, ✗ing, r, s
stick	ing, er, -insect, s	**straight*** (not bent)	er, est, ly, ness
stick y	ier, iest, ily, iness	**straighten**	ed, ing, er, s
stickleback	s	**strain**	ed, ing, er, s
stiff	er, est, ly, ness	**strait*** (sea channel)	s
stiffen	ed, ing, er, s	**strand**	ed, ing, s
stifle	d, ✗ing, r, s	**strange**	r, st, ly, ness
stile* (steps)	s	**stranger**	s
still	ed, ing, ness, s	**strangle**	d, ✗ing, hold, r, s
sting	ing, er, s	**strap**	ped, ping, less, s
stinging-nettle	s	**straw**	board, -coloured, -hat, s
stir	red, ring, rer, s	**strawberr** y	ies
stirrup	s	**stray**	ed, ing, er, s
stitch	ed, ing, es	**streak**	ed, ing, er, s
stoat	s	**streak** y	ier, iest, ily, iness
stock	ed, ing, ist, -car, -pot, -room, s	**stream**	ed, ing, lined, er, s
stocking	s	**street**	-sweeper, s
stockade	d, ✗ing, s	**strength**	s
stoke	d, ✗ing, r, s	**strengthen**	ed, ing, er, s
stole	n	**strenuous**	ly, ness
stomach	-ache, -pump, s	**stretch**	ed, ing, es
stone	d, ✗ing, -cold, -deaf, -mason, s	**stretcher**	-bearer, s
ston y	ier, iest, ily, iness	**strict**	er, est, ly, ness
stood		**stride**	✗ing, r, s

✗ Drop **e** before adding *ing*

strike	ℓing, r, s			
string	ing, -bag, -vest, s		**su**	
strip	ped, ping, per, -lighting, s		**subject**	ed, ing, s
stripe	d, ℓing, s		**submarine**	r, s
strode			**submerge**	d, ℓing, s
stroke	d, ℓing, r, s		**submit**	ted, ting, s
stroll	ed, ing, er, s		**subscribe**	d, ℓing, r, s
strong	er, est, ly, ish, hold, -room		**subscription**	s
struck			**subside**	d, ℓing, s
structure	s		**substance**	s
struggle	d, ℓing, r, s		**substantial**	ly
strum	med, ming, mer, s		**substitute**	d, ℓing, s
strung			**subtract**	ed, ing, ion, s
strut	ted, ting, ter, s		**suburb**	s
stub	bed, bing, by, s		**succeed**	ed, ing, s
stubborn	ly, ness		**success**	es
stuck			**successful**	ly
stud	ded, ding, s		**succession**	s
student	s		**successor**	s
studio	s		**such**	like
studious	ly, ness		**suck**	ed, ing, er, s
study	ing		**suction**	-pump
studied	ies		**sudden**	ly, ness
stuff	ed, ing, er, s		**suds**	
stuffy	ier, iest, ily, iness		**suet**	-pudding, y
stumble	d, ℓing, r, s		**suffer**	ed, ing, er, s
stump	ed, ing, s		**sufficient**	ly
stumpy	ier, iest, ily, iness		**suffocate**	d, ℓing, s
stun	ned, ning, ner, s		**suffocation**	
stung			**sugar**	ed, ing, y, -basin, -beet, -cane, s
stunt	ed, ing, man, men, s		**suggest**	ed, ing, ion, s
stupendous	ly, ness		**suicide**	s
stupid	ity, ly		**suit**	ed, ing, able, ably, ability, case, s
sturdy	ier, iest, ily, iness		**suite*** (set of furniture, rooms, etc.)	s
stutter	ed, ing, er, s		**sulk**	ed, ing, s
sty	ies		**sulk**y	ier, iest, ily, iness
style* (way; fashion)	d, ℓing, s		**sullen**	ly, ness
			sultana	s

ℓ Drop **e** before adding *ing*

*	style		suite
	stile		sweet

SW

sum* (add up; total) *med, ming, s*	**surplice*** (gown) *s*
summer *y, -time, -house, s*	**surplus*** (left over) *es*
summit *s*	**surprise** *d, øing, s*
summon *ed, ing, s*	**surrender** *ed, ing, s*
summons *es*	**surround** *ed, ing, s*
sumptuous *ly, ness*	**survey** *ed, ing, or, s*
sun* *ned, ning, beam, light, flower, s*	**survival**
sun* *-glasses, rise, set, shine, shade, s*	**survive** *d, øing, s*
sunn *y* *ier, iest, ily, iness*	**survivor** *s*
sunbathe *d, øing, r, s*	**suspect** *ed, ing, s*
sunburn *ed, t*	**suspend** *ed, ing, er, s*
sundae* (ice cream) *s*	**suspense**
Sunday* *-school, s*	**suspicion** *s*
sung	**suspicious** *ly, ness*
sunk *en*	**sustain** *ed, ing, s*
superb *ly*	
superintend *ed, ing, ent, s*	
superior *ity, s*	**SW**
supermarket *s*	**swagger** *ed, ing, er, -cane, -coat, -stick, s*
superstition *s*	**swallow** *ed, ing, er, s*
superstitious *ly, ness*	**swam**
supervise *d, øing, s*	**swamp** *ed, ing, s*
supervision	**swamp** *y* *ier, iest, ily, iness*
supervisor *s*	**swan** *s*
supper *-time, s*	**swap** or **swop** *ped, ping, per, s*
supple *ness*	**swarm** *ed, ing, s*
supply *ing*	**swarth** *y* *ier, iest, ily, iness*
suppl *ied* *ier, ies*	**sway** *ed, ing, s*
support *ed, ing, er, s*	**swear** *ing, er, -word, s*
suppose *d, øing, s*	**sweat** *ed, ing, y, er, -band, -shirt, -suit, s*
sure* (certain) *r, st, ly, ness, -footed*	**swede** *s*
surf* (sea foam) *ing, -board, -riding*	**sweep** *ing, er, stake, s*
surface *d, øing, s*	**swept**
surge *d, øing, s*	**sweet*** *er, est, ish, ly, ness, heart, -pea, s*
surgeon *s*	**sweeten** *ed, ing, er, s*
surger *y* *ies*	**swell** *ed, ing, s*
surname *s*	**swelter** *ed, ing, s*

é Drop **e** before adding *ing*

* sum	sun	sundae	sure	surf	surplice	sweet
some	son	Sunday	shore	serf	surplus	suite

sy

ta

swept	
swerve	d, ǿing, s
swift	er, est, ly, ness, s
swill	ed, ing, s
swim	mer, suit, s
swimming	-bath, -pool
swindle	d, ǿing, r, s
swine	herd. **swine**
swing	ing, er, s
swipe	d, ǿing, r, s
swirl	ed, ing, s
swish	ed, ing, es
switch	ed, ing, es
swivel	led, ling, s
swollen	
swoon	ed, ing, s
swoop	ed, ing, s
swop or **swap**	ped, ping, per, s
sword	sman, smen, -dance, s
swordfish	es or **swordfish**
swore	
sworn	
swum	
swung	

sy

sycamore	-tree, s
sympathetic	ally
sympathize	d, ǿing, r, s
sympath y	ies
symphon y	ies
symptom	s
synagogue	s
syringe	d, ǿing, s
syrup	y
system	atic, atically, s

ǿ Drop **e** before adding *ing*

ta

tabby-cat	s
table	-tennis, -cloth, -mat, s
table-spoon	ful, s
tableau	x or s
tablet	s
tack	ed, ing, s
tackle	d, ǿing, r, s
tact	ful, fully, less, lessly
tactics	
tadpole	s
tag	ged, ging, s
tail*	ed, ing, -end, -lamp, -light, -spin, s
tailor	ed, ing, -made, s
take	n, ǿing, r, -away, -off, s
talcum powder	
tale* (story)	-bearer, -teller, s
talent	ed, s
talk	ative, ed, ing, er, s
tall	er, est, ish, ness
tambourine	s
tame	d, ǿing, r, st, ly, ness, s
tamper	ed, ing, er, s
tan	ned, ning, ner, s
tandem	s
tangerine	s
tangle	d, ǿing, s
tango	ed, ing, s
tank	er, ful, -trap, s
tankard	s
tantalize	d, ǿing, s
tantrum	s
tap	ped, ping, per, -dance, -dancing, s
tape	d, ǿing, s
tape	-measure, -recorder, -recording, s
tapestr y	ies
tapioca	

* tail
* tale

te

tar	red, ring, ry, s
tarantula	s
tare* (weed)	s
target	s
tarnish	ed, ing, es
tarpaulin	s
tart	let, s
tartan	s
task	ed, ing, master, s
tassel	s
taste	d, øing, r, s
tasteful	ly, ness
tasteless	ly, ness
tatter	ed, ing, s
tattoo	ed, ing, er, ist, -mark, s
taught* (teach)	
taunt	ed, ing, er, s
taut* (tight)	er, est, ly, ness
tavern	s
tax	ation, ed, ing, es
taxi	-cab, -driver, -rank, s

te

tea*	cake, -cloth, cup, pot, -service, s
tea*	-set, -things, -time, table, -tray, s
tea-cos y	ies
tea-leaf	-leaves
tea-part y	ies
tea-spoon	ful, s
teach	ing, ings, es
teacher	s
teak	
team* (side; number)	-work, s
tear* (pull apart)	ing, s
tear	-gas, -drop, s
tearful	ly, ness

tease	d, øing, r, s
technical	ly
technician	s
Teddy bear	s
tedious	ly, ness
tee* (golf)	d, ing, -shot, s
tee-shirt or T-shirt	s
teem* (pour; swarm)	ed, ing, s
teenage	d, -boy, -girl
teenager	s
teeth	
telegram	s
telegraph	ed, ing, -line, -pole, -wire, s
telephone	d, øing, s
telescope	d, øing, s
televise	d, øing, s
television	s
tell	ing, er, -tale, s
temper	ed, ing, s
temperature	s
temple	s
temporar y	ily
tempt	ation, ed, ing, er, s
tend	ed, ing, s
tender	-hearted, ly, ness
tenement	s
tennis	-ball, -court, -racket
tenor	s
tense	d, øing, r, st, ly, ness, s
tent	-peg, -pole, -rope, s
tentacle	s
tepid	ly, ness
term	ly, ed, ing, s
terminus	es or termini
terrace	d, øing, -house, s
terrible	ness
terribly	

ø Drop **e** before adding *ing*

*				
	tare	taught	tea	team
	tear	taut	tee	teem

th

terrier	*s*	**thermometer**	*s*
terrific	*ally*	**thermos flask**	*s*
terrify	*ing*	**these**	
terrif *ied*	*ies*	**they**	
territorial	*s*	**they'll** (they will; they shall)	
territor *y*	*ies*	**they're*** (they are)	
terror *ism, ist, -stricken, s*		**they've** (they have)	
terrorize	*d, ∉ing, s*	**thick** *er, est, ly, ness, ish, -skinned*	
test *ed, ing, -paper, -piece, -tube, s*		**thicken** *ed, ing, er, s*	
testament	*s*	**thicket**	*s*
testimonial	*s*	**thief**	**thieves**
tetanus		**thieve** *d, ∉ing, s*	
tether	*ed, ing, s*	**thimble** *ful, s*	
text	*-book, s*	**thin** *ned, ning, ner, nest, ly, ness, s*	
textile	*s*	**thing**	*s*
		think *ing, er, s*	
		thirst *ed, ing, s*	
		thirst *y* *ier, iest, ily, iness*	

th

than		**this**	
thank *ed, ing, -offering, s*		**thistle**	*s*
thankful *ly, ness*		**thorn**	*s*
thankless *ly, ness*		**thorn** *y* *ier, iest, ily, iness*	
that		**thorough** *ly, ness, bred, fare*	
that's (that is)		**those**	
thatch *ed, ing, es*		**though**	
thaw *ed, ing, s*		**thought** *-reader, s*	
theatre *-ticket, s*		**thoughtful** *ly, ness*	
theatrical *ly, s*		**thoughtless** *ly, ness*	
theft *s*		**thrash** *ed, ing, ings, es*	
their* (belonging to them)		**thread** *ed, ing, bare, er, s*	
theirs* (belonging to them)		**threat** *s*	
them *selves*		**threaten** *ed, ing, s*	
then		**thresh** *ed, ing, es*	
theor *y* *ies*		**threw*** (throw)	
there* (in that place) *abouts, after*		**thrift** *less*	
therefore		**thrift** *y* *ier, iest, ily, iness*	
there's* (there is)		**thrill** *ed, ing, er, s*	

∉ Drop **e** before adding *ing*

*	their	theirs	threw
	there	there's	through
	they're		

ti

to

thrive	d, e̅ing, s
throat	s
throb	bed, bing, s
throne* (king's seat)	s
throng	ed, ing, s
throttle	d, e̅ing, s
through* (from end to end)	out
throw	ing, er, n,* s
thrush	es
thrust	ing, s
thud	ded, ding, s
thug	s
thumb	ed, ing, -mark, -nail, screw, s
thump	ed, ing, er, s
thunder	ed, ing, y, bolt, clap, storm, s
Thursday	s

ti

tiara	s
tick	ed, ing, s
ticket	-collector, -office, s
tickle	d, e̅ing, r, s
ticklish	ly, ness
tide* (sea)	-mark, s
tidings	
tidy	ing
tid ied	ier, iest, ily, iness, ies
tie	d,* -clip, -pin, s
tying	
tiger	-cat, -moth, s
tigress	es
tight	er, est, ly, ness, -rope, s
tighten	ed, ing, er, s
tile	d, e̅ing, r, s
till	ed, ing, er, s
till or until	

tilt	ed, ing, er, s
timber	ed, -mill, -yard, s
time	d, e̅ing, r, ly, less, -bomb, table, s
timid	ity, ly, ness
tin	ned, ning, ny, -opener, foil, -tack, s
tinge	d, e̅ing, s
tingle	d, e̅ing, s
tinker	ed, ing, s
tinkle	d, e̅ing, s
tinsel	led, ling, ly
tint	ed, ing, s
tin y	ier, iest, ily, iness
tip	ped, ping, per, ster, s
tiptoe	d, ing, s
tire* (weary)	d, e̅ing, some, s
tired	ness
tireless	ly, ness
tissue	-paper, s
title	d, s
titter	ed, ing, s

to

to* (towards)	
toad	-in-the-hole, s
toadstool	s
to and fro	
toast	ed, ing, er, -rack, s
tobacco	nist, -pipe, -plant, s
toboggan	ed, ing, er, s
today or to-day	
toddle	d, e̅ing, r, s
toe*	d, ing, -cap, -hold, -nail, s
toffee	-apple, s
together	ness
toil	ed, ing, er, s
toilet	-paper, -roll, -soap, s

e̅ Drop e before adding ing

*	throne	through	tide	tire	toe	to
	thrown	threw	tied	tyre	tow	too
						two (2)

token	*s*	toss	*ed, ing, es*
told		total	*led, ling, ly, s*
tolerate	*d, ǝing, s*	totter	*ed, ing, y, er, s*
toll	*ed, ing, -bridge, -gate, s*	touch	*ed, ing, y, es*
tomahawk	*s*	tough	*er, est, ly, ness, s*
tomato	*es*	toughen	*ed, ing, s*
tomb	*stone, s*	tour	*ed, ing, ist, s*
tomcat	*s*	tournament	*s*
tomorrow or to-morrow	*s*	tousle	*d, ǝing, s*
tomtit	*s*	tow* (pull)	*ed, ing, -line, -path, -rope, s*
ton or tonne (metric)	*s*	towards or toward	
tone	*d, ǝing, -deaf, s*	towel	*led, ling, -rail, s*
tongs		tower	*ed, ing, -block, s*
tongue	*-tied, -twister, s*	town	*-council, -crier, -hall, s*
tonic	*s*	toy	*ed, ing, shop, s*
tonight or to-night			
tonsil	*s*		
tonsillitis			**tr**
too* (more than enough; also)			
took		trace	*d, ǝing, r, s*
tool	*-bag, -chest, -shed, s*	tracing-paper	
tooth	*ache, paste, powder, less,* **teeth**	track	*ed, ing, er, suit, s*
tooth-brush	*es*	tractor	*s*
top	*ped, ping, per, knot, -heavy, -hat, s*	trade	*d, ǝing, mark, sman, smen, r, s*
topic	*s*	traffic	*-sign, -signal, -lights*
topple	*d, ǝing, s*	traged *y*	*ies*
topsy-turvy		tragic	*ally*
torch	*es*	trail	*ed, ing, er, s*
tore		train	*ed, ing, er, s*
torment	*ed, ing, or, s*	traitor	*ous, ously, s*
torn		tramp	*ed, ing, er, s*
tornado	*es*	trample	*d, ǝing, r, s*
torpedo	*ed, ing, es*	trampoline	*s*
torrent	*s*	transfer	*red, ring, able, s*
torrential	*ly*	transform	*ed, ing, ation, s*
tortoise	*-shell, s*	transistor	*-radio, s*
torture	*d, ǝing, r, -chamber, s*	translate	*d, ǝing, s*
		translation	*s*

ǝ Drop **e** before adding *ing*

* too
to
two (2)

tow
toe

transparent	*ly, ness*	**trim**	*med, ming, mer, mest, ly, ness, s*	
transport	*ed, ing, er, ation, able, s*	**trinket**	*s*	
trap	*ped, ping, per, -door, s*	**trio**	*s*	
trapeze	*s*	**trip**	*ped, ping, per, s*	
travel	*led, ling, ler, s*	**triple**	*d, ɇing, s*	
trawl	*ed, ing, er, s*	**triplet**	*s*	
tray	*-cloth, ful, s*	**tripod**	*s*	
treacherous	*ly, ness*	**triumph**	*ed, ing, ant, antly, s*	
treacher *y*	*ies*	**trod**	*den*	
treacle		**trolley**	*s*	
tread	*ing, s*	**trombone**	*ɇist, s*	
treason	*able*	**troop*** (of scouts, soldiers)	*ed, ing, er, s*	
treasure	*d, ɇing, r, -chest, -hunt, s*	**troph** *y*	*ies*	
treat	*ed, ing, ment, s*	**tropic**	*al, ally, s*	
treble	*d, ɇing, s*	**trot**	*ted, ting, ter, s*	
tree *-stump, -top, -trunk, s*		**trouble**	*d, ɇing, some, -maker, s*	
trek	*ked, king, ker, s*	**trough**	*s*	
trellis	*-work*	**troupe*** (of entertainers)	*r, s*	
tremble	*d, ɇing, s*	**trousers**		
tremendous	*ly, ness*	**trousseau**	*x or s*	
trench	*es*	**trout**	**trout**	
trespass	*ed, ing, es*	**trowel**	*s*	
trespasser	*s*	**truant**	*s*	
trestle	*-table, s*	**truck**	*-load, s*	
trial	*s*	**trudge**	*d, ɇing, s*	
triangle	*s*	**true**	*r, st, ness*	
tribe	*sman, smen, s*	**truly**		
tributar *y*	*ies*	**trumpet**	*ed, ing, er, -call, s*	
trick	*ed, ing, ery, ster, s*	**truncheon**	*s*	
trick *y*	*ier, iest, ily, iness*	**trunk**	*s*	
trickle	*d, ɇing, s*	**truss**	*ed, ing, es*	
tricycle	*d, ɇing, s*	**trust**	*ed, ing, worthy, s*	
tried		**trust** *y*	*ier, iest, ily, iness*	
trier	*s*	**truth**	*s*	
tries		**truthful**	*ly, ness*	
trifle	*d, ɇing, s*	**try**	*ing*	
trigger	*ed, ing, s*	**tr** *ied*	*ier, ies*	

ɇ Drop **e** before adding *ing*

*   troop
     troupe

tu

tuba	s
tubby	ier, iest, iness
tube	øing, less, -train, s
tuck	ed, ing, -shop, s
Tudor	s
Tuesday	s
tuft	s
tug	ged, ging, ger, boat, s
tug-of-war	
tuition	
tulip	s
tumble	d, øing, r, down, -dryer, s
tumbler	ful, s
tumult	s
tumultuous	ly, ness
tundra	s
tune	d, øing, r, s
tuneful	ly, ness
tuneless	ly, ness
tunic	s
tunnel	led, ling, ler, s
turban	s
turbine	s
turf	ed, ing, s or **turves**
turkey	cock, s
Turkish delight	
turmoil	
turn	ed, ing, er, over, stile, table, s
turnip	s
turpentine	
turquoise	s
turret	ed, s
turtle	-neck, -shell, -soup, -dove, s
tusk	s
tussle	d, øing, s
tutor	ial, s

tw

twang	ed, ing, s
tweed	s
tweezers	
twice	
twiddle	d, øing, r, s
twig	s
twilight	
twin	ned, ning, -brother, -sister, s
twine	d, øing, s
twinge	d, øing, s
twinkle	d, øing, s
twirl	ed, ing, s
twist	ed, ing, er, s
twisty	ier, iest, ily, iness
twitch	ed, ing, es
twitter	ed, ing, s

ty

tying	
type	d, øing, written, writing, writer, s
typist	s
typhoon	s
typical	ly, ness
tyrannize	d, øing, s
tyrant	s
tyre* (wheel cover)˙	s

ug

ugly	ier, iest, ily, iness

um

umbrella	-stand, s
umpire	d, øing, s

ø Drop **e** before adding *ing*

* tyre
  tire

un

un	
unable	
unafraid	
unaided	
unarm	*ed, ing, s*
unattractive	*ly, ness*
unavoidable	*y*
unaware	*s*
unbalance	*d, e̸ing, s*
unbearable	*y*
unbeaten	
unbolt	*ed, ing, s*
unbuckle	*d, e̸ing, s*
unbutton	*ed, ing, s*
uncanny	*ily, iness*
uncertain	*ly, ty*
uncivilized	
uncle	*s*
unclean	*liness*
uncomfortable	*ness*
uncommon	*ly, ness*
unconscious	*ly, ness*
uncork	*ed, ing, s*
uncover	*ed, ing, s*
uncurl	*ed, ing, s*
undamaged	
undecided	*ly*
under	*clothes, clothing, wear*
under	*go, going, goes, gone, went*
undercurrent	*s*
underground	
undergrowth	
underneath	
understand	*able, ing, s*
understood	
understudy	*ing*
understudied	*ies*

undertake	*n, e̸ing, r, s*
undertook	
undid	
undo	*ing*
undone	
undoubted	*ly*
undress	*ed, ing, es*
uneasy	*ier, iest, ily, iness*
unemployed	*ment*
uneven	*ly, ness*
unexpected	*ly, ness*
unexplored	
unfair	*ly, ness*
unfasten	*ed, ing, s*
unfinished	
unfit	*ted, ting, s*
unfold	*ed, ing, s*
unfortunate	*ly*
unfriendly	*iness*
unfurnished	
ungrateful	*ly, ness*
unguarded	*ly, ness*
unhappy	*ier, iest, ily, iness*
unharmed	
unhealthy	*ier, iest, ily, iness*
unhurt	
uniform	*ed, s*
unimportant	
uninhabited	
uninjured	
uninteresting	
Union Jack	*s*
unite	*d, e̸ing, s*
universe	
university	*ies*
unjust	*ly, ness*
unkind	*er, est, ly, ness*

e̸ Drop **e** before adding *ing*

up ur us

unknown	
unlawful	*ly, ness*
unless	
unlike	*ness*
unlikel *y*	*ier, iest, ihood*
unload	*ed, ing, s*
unlock	*ed, ing, s*
unluck *y*	*ier, iest, ily, iness*
unmistakabl *e*	*y*
unnecessar *y*	*ily*
unoccupied	
unpack	*ed, ing, s*
unpleasant	*ly, ness*
unpopular	*ity, ly*
unravel	*led, ling, s*
unreasonabl *e*	*y*
unreliable	*ness*
unroll	*ed, ing, s*
unsaddle	*d, ø̸ing, s*
unsafe	*r, st, ly, ness*
unscrew	*ed, ing, s*
unselfish	*ly, ness*
unstead *y*	*ier, iest, ily, iness*
unsuitable	
untangle	*d, ø̸ing, s*
untid *y*	*ier, iest, ily, iness*
untie	*d, s*
untying	
until or till	
untrue	
unusual	*ly, ness*
unveil	*ed, ing, s*
unwelcome	
unwell	
unwilling	*ly, ness*
unwise	*ly*
unwrap	*ped, ping, s*

up

upbringing	
upheaval	*s*
upholster	*ed, ing, er, s*
upholster *y*	*ies*
upkeep	
upon	
upper	*most, -cut, s*
upright	*ly, ness, s*
uprising	*s*
uproar	*s*
uproot	*ed, ing, s*
upset	*ting, s*
upside-down	
upstairs	
upstream	
upturn	*ed, ing, s*
upward	*ly, s*

ur

uranium	
urban	
urchin	*s*
urge	*d, ø̸ing, s*
urgenc *y*	*ies*
urgent	*ly*
urn* (vase; tea-urn)	*s*

us

use	*d, ø̸ing, r, s*
useful	*ly, ness*
useless	*ly, ness*
usher	*ed, ing, s*
usherette	*s*
usual	*ly, ness*

ø̸ Drop **e** before adding *ing*

* urn
   earn

ut

utensil	s
utmost	
utter	ed, ing, ance, s
utter	ly, most, ness

va

vacanc y	ies
vacant	ly
vacate	d, ǿing, s
vacation	s
vaccinate	d, ǿing, s
vacuum	-cleaner, -flask, s
vague	r, st, ly, ness
vain* (proud)	er, est, ly
vale* (valley)	s
valentine	s
valiant	ly
valley	s
valuable	s
value	d, ǿing, less, r, s
valve	s
vane* (weathercock)	s
vanilla	
vanish	ed, ing, es
vanit y	ies
vanquish	ed, ing, es
variet y	ies
various	ly, ness
varnish	ed, ing, es
vary	ing
var ied	ies
vase	s
vaseline	
vast	er, est, ly, ness
vault	ed, ing, er, s

ve

veal	
vegetable	s
vegetarian	s
vegetation	
vehicle	s
veil* (a covering)	ed, ing, s
vein* (blood-vessel)	ed, ing, s
velvet	y, s
vengeance	
venison	
vent	ed, ing, -hole, s
ventilate	d, ǿing, s
ventilation	
ventilator	s
ventriloquist	s
venture	d, ǿing, some, s
veranda(h)	s
verb	al, ally, s
verdict	s
verge	d, ǿing, s
verger	s
vermilion	s
vermin	ous, ously
verse	s
version	s
versus	
vertical	ly
very	
vessel	s
vest	s
vestibule	s
vestr y	ies
vet	ted, ting, s
veteran	s
veterinar y	ies
vex	ed, ing, es, ation, atious

ǿ Drop e before adding ing

*	vain	vale
	vane	veil
	vein	

vi   vo vu wa

vi	
viaduct	s
vibrate	d, ℓing, s
vibration	s
vicar	age, s
vice	-admiral, -captain, s
vicious	ly, ness
victim	s
victor	s
victorious	ly, ness
victory	ies
victual	led, ling, ler, s
videotape	d, ℓing, s
view	ed, ing, er, point, s
vigorous	ly, ness
vigour	
viking	s
vile	r, st, ly, ness
villa	s
village	r, s
villain* (scoundrel)	ous, ously, s
villein* (serf)	s
vine	yard, s
vinegar	y
violence	
violent	ly
violet	s
violin	ist, s
virtue	s
visible	y
visibility	
vision	s
visit	ed, ing, or, s
vital	ity, ly
vivarium	s or vivaria
vivid	ly, ness
vixen	s

vo	
vocabulary	ies
vocalist	s
voice	d, ℓing, s
volcano	es
vole	s
volley	ēd, ing, -ball, s
volt	age, s
volume	s
voluntary	ily
volunteer	ed, ing, s
vomit	ed, ing, s
vote	d, ℓing, r, s
vouch	ed, ing, es
voucher	s
vow	ed, ing, s
vowel	s
voyage	d, ℓing, r, s

vu	
vulgar	ity, ly
vulnerable	ness
vulture	s

wa	
waddle	d, ℓing, r, s
wade	d, ℓing, r, s
wafer	s
waft	ed, ing, er, s
wag	ged, ging, ger, s
wage	d, ℓing, r, -earner, s
waggle	d, ℓing, r, s
wagon or waggon	er, -load, s
waif	s
wail	ed, ing, er, s

ℓ Drop e before adding *ing*

*   villain
      villein

we

waist* (of body)	coat, s
wait* (stay; serve)	ed, ing, s
waiter	s
waitress	es
waiting-room	s
wake	d, ẹing, r, s
waken	ed, ing, er, s
walk	ed, ing, er, s
walking-stick	s
wall	ed, ing, chart, flower, paper, s
wallet	s
wallow	ed, ing, er, s
walnut	-tree, s
walrus	es
waltz	ed, ing, es
wand	s
wander	ed, ing, er, s
wangle	d, ẹing, r, s
want	ed, ing, s
war*	-dance, -paint, -path, ship, s
war-cr y	ies
warrior	s
warble	d, ẹing, r, s
ward	ed, ing, en, er, s
wardrobe	s
ware* (goods)	house, s
warm	th, ed, ing, er, est, ish, ly, s
warn* (be careful)	ed, ing, er, s
warp	ed, ing, s
warrant	ed, ing, s
warren	s
wart	s
war y	ier, iest, ily, iness
wash	able, ed, ing, es
washer	s
wasn't (was not)	
wasp	s

waste*	d, ẹing, land, -bin, -paper, -pipe, s
wasteful	ly, ness
watch	ed, ing, man, men, es
watchful	ly, ness
water	ed, ing, -colour, cress, fall, proof, s
water-lil y	ies
water y	ier, iest, ily, iness
wave	d, ẹing, s
waver	ed, ing, er, s
wav y	ier, iest, ily, iness
wax	ed, ing, en, es, works
wax y	ier, iest, ily, iness
way* (direction; manner; road)	lay, side, s

we

weak* (not strong)	er, est, ly, ness, -kneed
weaken	ed, ing, s
weakling	s
wealth	
wealth y	ier, iest, ily, iness
weapon	s
wear* (dressed in)	ing, er, s
weary	ing
wear ied	ier, iest, ily, iness, ies
weasel	s
weather*	ed, ing, cock, -forecast, -vane, s
weave	d, ẹing, r, s
we'd (we had; we should; we would)	
wed	ded, ding, s
wedding	-cake, -card, -day, -ring, -bell, s
wedding-dress	es
wedge	d, ẹing, s
Wednesday	s
weed	ed, ing, er, -killer, s
weed y	ier, iest, iness
week* (seven days)	-day, -end, s

ẹ Drop **e** before adding ing

waist	wait	war	ware	warn	way	weak	weather
waste	weight	wore	wear	worn	weigh	week	whether

wh

weekl y *ies*	**where** *abouts, as, by, fore, upon*
weep *ing, y, er, s*	**wherever**
wept	**whether*** (if)
weigh* (measure heaviness) *ed, ing, s*	**which*** (what one? who?) *ever*
weight* (heaviness) *ed, ing, -lifter, s*	**whiff** *ed, ing, s*
weight y *ier, iest, ily, iness*	**while** *d, ∉ing, s*
weir *s*	**whilst**
weird *er, est, ly, ness*	**whimper** *ed, ing, er, s*
welcome *d, ∉ing, s*	**whine*** (cry; wail) *d, ∉ing, r, s*
weld *ed, ing, er, s*	**whip** *ped, ping, per, s*
welfare	**whippet** *s*
well *-behaved, -bred, -wisher, s*	**whirl** *ed, ing, igig, pool, wind, s*
we'll (we shall; we will)	**whisk** *ed, ing, er, s*
wellington boot *s*	**whisker** *ed, y, s*
went	**whisk** y *ies*
wept	**whisper** *ed, ing, er, s*
we're (we are)	**whist** *-drive*
were	**whistle** *d, ∉ing, r, s*
weren't (were not)	**white** *r, st, ly, ness, s*
west *ern, erly, ward, wards*	**whiten** *ed, ing, er, s*
wet *ted, ting, ter, test, ly, ness, s*	**whitewash** *ed, ing, es*
we've (we have)	**whiting** *s* or **whiting**
	Whit Sunday *s*
	Whitsun *tide*
wh	**whiz** *zes* or **whizz** *ed, ing, es*
whack *ed, ing, s*	**who** *ever*
whale *∉ing, r, bone, -boat, s*	**who'd** (who had; who would)
wharf *s* or **wharves**	**who'll** (who will; who shall)
what *ever, soever*	**who're** (who are)
what's (what is)	**who's*** (who is)
wheat *-field, -flour, germ, s*	**whom** *soever*
wheedle *d, ∉ing, r, s*	**whole*** (all; complete) *sale, some*
wheel *ed, ing, er, barrow, -chair, s*	**wholly*** (completely)
wheeze *d, ∉ing, s*	**whoop** *ed, ing, s*
whelk *s*	**whortleberr** y *ies*
when *ever*	**whose*** (belonging to whom)
whence	**why**

∉ Drop **e** before adding *ing*

*	weigh	weight	whether	which	whine	who's	whole	wholly
	way	wait	weather	witch	wine	whose	hole	holy

wi

wo

wi

wicked	er, est, ly, ness
wicker	work
wicket	-keeper, s
wide	r, st, ly, spread, s
widen	ed, ing, er, s
width	s
widow	ed, ing, er, s
wield	ed, ing, er, s
wife	ly, **wives**
wiggle	d, øing, r, s
wigwam	s
wild	er, est, ly, ness, life, fowl, fire, s
wilderness	es
wilful	ly, ness
will	ed, ing, -power, s
willing	ly, ness
willow	-herb, -tree, -warbler, s
wil y	ier, iest, ily, iness
win	ning, ner, s
wince	d, øing, s
wind (turn; twist)	ing, er, s
wind	ed, ing, -chart, fall, mill, ward, s
wind y	ier, iest, ily, iness
window	-cleaner, -ledge, -pane, -sill, s
windscreen	-wiper, s
wine* (a drink)	d, øing, -bottle, cask, s
wlng	ed, ing, er, -span, s
wink	ed, ing, er, s
winkle	d, øing, s
winter	ed, ing, -time, s
wintr y	ier, iest, ily, iness
wipe	d, øing, r, s
wire	d, øing, -netting, -rope, -cutter, s
wireless	ed, ing, es
wir y	ier, iest, ily, iness
wisdom	-tooth, -teeth

wo

wise	r, st, ly
wish	ed, ing, es
wishful	ly, ness
wistful	ly, ness
wit	ted, less, s
witt y	ier, iest, ily, iness
witch* (old woman)	es, craft, -hunt
with	in, out
withdraw	al, ing, n, s
withdrew	
wither	ed, ing, s
withstand	ing, s
withstood	
witness	ed, ing, -box, es
wizard	ry, s
wizened	

wobble	d, øing, r, s
woe	begone, s
woeful	ly, ness
woke	n
wolf	-cub, -pack, **wolves**
woman	hood, ly, **women**
won* (win)	
wonder	ed, ing, ment, land, s
wonderful	ly, ness
won't (will not)	
wood*	ed, man, men, -cutter, land, s
wooden	ly, ness
wood-louse	-lice
woodpecker	s
woodwork	
wool	s
woollen	s
wooll y	ier, iest, iness, ies

é Drop **e** before adding *ing*

*	wine	witch	won	wood
	whine	which	one (1)	would

wr   x   ya   ye

word *ed, ing, s*	**write*** (form letters) *r, s*
wore* (wear)	**writing** *-case, -desk, -paper, -table, s*
work *ed, ing, man, men, shop, er, s*	**written**
world *-famous, -wide, s*	**writhe** *d, ∉ing, s*
worm *ed, ing, y, eaten, -cast, -hole, s*	**wrong** *ed, ing, ful, ly, ness, s*
worn* (wear) *-out*	**wrote**
worry *ing*	**wrung*** (twisted)
worr *ied* *ier, ies, isome*	**wry** *er, est, ly, ness*
worse	
worsen *˙ed, ing, s*	
worst	**x**
worship *ped, ping, per, s*	**X-ray** *ed, ing, s*
worth *while*	**xylophone** *s*
worthless *ly, ness*	
worth *y ier, iest, ily, iness, ies*	
would* (past of will)	**ya**
wouldn't (would not)	**yacht** *ing, sman, smen, -club, s*
wound (turned; twisted)	**yak** *s*
wound (injure) *ed, ing, s*	**yap** *ped, ping, per, s*
wove *n*	**yard** *age, stick, s*
	yarn *ed, ing, s*
	yawn *ed, ing, s*
wr	
wrangle *d, ∉ing, r, s*	
wrap* (cover) *ped, ping, per, s*	**ye**
wrath *ful, fully*	**year** *ly, ling, s*
wreath *s*	**yearn** *ed, ing, s*
wreck *age, ed, ing, er, s*	**yeast** *y*
wren *s*	**yell** *ed, ing, er, s*
wrench *ed, ing, es*	**yellow** *er, est, ness, ish, y, s*
wrestle *d, ∉ing, r, s*	**yelp** *ed, ing, er, s*
wretch *es*	**yeo** *man* *men*
wretched *ly, ness*	**yes** *es*
wriggle *d, ∉ing, r, s*	**yesterday** *s*
wring* (twist) *ing, er, s*	**yet**
wrinkle *d, ∉ing, r, s*	**yeti** *s*
wrist *let, band, s*	**yew*** *-tree, s*

*∉ Drop **e** before adding ing*

*****	wore	worn	would	wrap	wring	write	wrung	yew
	war	warn	wood	rap	ring	right	rung	you
								ewe

yi

yield	*ed, ing, s*

yo

yodel	*led, ling, ler, s*
yoga	
yog(h)urt	
yoke* (wooden bar; join)	*d, ėing, s*
yokel	*s*
yolk* (of egg)	*s*
yonder	
Yorkshire pudding	*s*
you* (person)	
you'd (you had; you would)	
you'll (you will)	
you're (you are)	
you've (you have)	
young	*er, est, ish*
youngster	*s*
your	
yours	
your *self*	*selves*
youth	*-club, s*
youthful	*ly, ness*
yowl	*ed, ing, er, s*
yule	*-log, tide, s*

ze

zeal	
zealous	*ly*
zebra	*s*
zebu	*s*
zephyr	*s*
zero	*s*
zest	*ful, fully*

zi

zigzag	*ged, ging, s*
zinc	
zip	*ped, ping, per, -fastener, s*
zither	*s*

zo

zodiac	
zone	*d, ėing, s*
zoo	*s*
zoological garden	*s*
zoologist	*s*
zoology	
zoom	*ed, ing, s*

zu

Zulu	*s*

ė Drop **e** before adding *ing*

*	yoke	you
	yolk	yew
		ewe

Boys' Names

A
Aaron
Adam
Adrian
Alan
Alexander
Alistair
Alfred
Allan
Andrew
Angus
Anthony
Antony
Arthur
Ashley

B
Barry
Benjamin
Bernard
Brendan
Brian
Bryan
Bruce

C
Calvin
Carl
Cedric
Charles
Christian
Christopher
Clifford
Clive
Colin
Courtenay
Craig

D
Dale
Damian
Daniel
Darren
David
Dean
Dennis
Derek
Dominic
Donald
Duncan
Dylan

E
Edmund
Edward
Eric

F
Francis
Frank
Frederick

G
Gareth
Gary
Gavin
Geoffrey
George
Giles
Glen(n)
Glyn
Gordon
Graham
Gregory
Guy

H
Henry
Howard
Hugh

I
Ian
Ivan

J
James
Jamie
Jason
Jeffrey
Jeremy
Jocelyn
John
Jonathan
Joseph
Julian
Justin

K
Karl
Keith
Kenneth
Kevin

L
Lance
Laurence
Lawrence
Lee
Leon
Leonard
Leslie
Luke

M
Malcolm
Marc
Marcus
Mark
Martin
Martyn
Matthew
Maurice
Melvin
Mervyn
Michael
Miles

N
Nathan
Nathaniel
Neil
Neville
Nicholas
Nigel
Noel
Norman

O
Oliver
Owen

P
Patrick
Paul
Peter
Philip
Piers

Q
Quentin

R
Ralph
Randolph
Raymond
Reginald
Rex
Richard
Robert
Robin
Roderick
Rodney
Roger
Roland
Rolf
Ronald
Roy
Royston
Rufus
Rupert
Russell
Ryan

S
Samuel
Scott
Sebastian
Seán
Shane
Shaun
Sidney
Simon
Spencer
Stanley
Stephen
Steven
Stewart
Stuart

T
Terence
Terry
Thomas
Timothy
Tony
Trevor
Tristram

V
Vernon
Victor
Vincent
Vivian

W
Wallace
Walter
Warren
Wayne
Wilfred
William
Winston

Girls' Names

A
Abigail
Adele
Adrienne
Aileen
Alexandra
Alexis
Alice
Alison
Amanda
Amelia
Amy
Andrea
Angela
Anita
Ann(e)
Anna
Annabel
Annabella
Annette
Anthea
Antonia
April
Audra
Audrey
Averil

B
Barbara
Belinda
Beryl
Betty
Beverley
Blanche
Brenda
Bridget
Bryony

C
Cara
Carla
Carol(e)
Caroline
Carolyn
Carrie
Catherine
Cecilia
Celia
Charlotte
Charmaine
Cheryl
Chloe
Christine
Claire
Clare
Claudia
Colette
Corinne

D
Danielle
Daphne
Dawn
Debbie
Deborah
Debra
Deirdre
Delia
Della
Denise
Diana
Diane
Dionne
Donna
Dorothy

E
Eileen
Elaine
Eleanor
Elizabeth
Ellen
Emily
Emma
Enid
Erica
Esmé(e)
Estelle
Ester
Eveline
Evelyn

F
Fay(e)
Felicity
Fiona
Fleur
Frances

G
Gabrielle
Gail
Gayle
Gaynor
Gemma
Georgina
Geraldine
Germaine
Gillian
Gina
Glenda
Glynis
Gwyneth

H
Hannah
Hayley
Hazel
Heather
Heidi
Helen
Hilary
Holly

I
Irene
Isabel

J
Jacqueline
Jane
Janet
Janice
Janine
Jayne
Jean
Jeanette
Jennifer
Jessica
Jill
Joan
Joanna
Joanne
Johanna
Josephine
Joy
Judith
Julia
Julie
June
Justine

K
Karen
Kate
Katharine
Katherine
Kathleen
Kathryn
Katrina
Kay
Keeley
Kelly
Kerry
Kimberly
Kitty
Kirsten
Kirsty

L
Laura
Leanne
Lesley
Linda
Lindsey
Lisa
Lorna
Lorraine
Louisa
Louise
Lucy
Lyndsey
Lynn(e)

M
Madeleine
Mandy
Margaret
Maria

Marie
Martina
Mary
Matilda
Maureen
Maxine
Melanie
Melinda
Melissa
Merle
Michelle
Miranda

N
Nadia
Nadine
Nancy
Naomi
Natalie
Natasha
Nichola
Nicola
Nicole
Nina

O
Olivia

P
Pamela
Patricia
Paula
Pauline
Penelope
Penny
Philippa
Polly

R
Rachael
Rachel
Rebecca
Rebekah
Rita
Rosalie
Rosalind
Rosamund
Rose
Rosemary
Rowena
Ruth

S
Sadie
Sally
Sallyann
Samantha
Sandra
Sara(h)
Sharon
Sheila
Shelley
Shirley
Shona
Sonia
Sophie
Stacey
Stella
Stephanie
Susan
Susannah
Susanne
Suzanne
Sybil
Sylvia

T
Tamara
Tammy
Tamsin
Tania
Tanya
Tara
Teresa
Theresa
Tina
Tracey
Tracy

U
Ursula

V
Valerie
Vanessa
Vicki
Vicky
Victoria
Virginia
Vivien
Vivienne

W
Wendy

Y
Yolande
Yvonne

Z
Zara
Zelda
Zoe

Numbers

	Cardinal		Ordinal				Roman
1	one	s	first	ly,	s	1st	I
2	two	s	second	ly,	s	2nd	II
3	three	s	third	ly,	.s	3rd	III
4	four	s	fourth	ly,	s	4th	IV
5	five	s	fifth	ly,	s	5th	V
6	six	es	sixth	ly,	s	6th	VI
7	seven	s	seventh	ly,	s	7th	VII
8	eight	s	eighth	ly,	s	8th	VIII
9	nine	s	ninth	ly,	s	9th	IX
10	ten	s	tenth	ly,	s	10th	X
11	eleven	s	eleventh		s	11th	XI
12	twelve	s	twelfth		s	12th	XII
13	thirteen	s	thirteenth		s	13th	XIII
14	fourteen	s	fourteenth		s	14th	XIV
15	fifteen	s	fifteenth		s	15th	XV
16	sixteen	s	sixteenth		s	16th	XVI
17	seventeen	s	seventeenth		s	17th	XVII
18	eighteen	s	eighteenth		s	18th	XVIII
19	nineteen	s	nineteenth		s	19th	XIX
20	twent y	ies	twentieth		s	20th	XX
21	twenty-one	s	twenty-first		s	21st	XXI
22	twenty-two	s	twenty-second		s	22nd	XXII
23	twenty-three	s	twenty-third		s	23rd	XXIII
24	twenty-four	s	twenty-fourth		s	24th	XXIV
25	twenty-five	s	twenty-fifth		s	25th	XXV
26	twenty-six	es	twenty-sixth		s	26th	XXVI
27	twenty-seven	s	twenty-seventh		s	27th	XXVII
28	twenty-eight	s	twenty-eighth		s	28th	XXVIII
29	twenty-nine	s	twenty-ninth		s	29th	XXIX
30	thirt y	ies	thirtieth		s	30th	XXX
31	thirty-one	s	thirty-first		s	31st	XXXI
40	fort y	ies	fortieth		s	40th	XL
41	forty-one	s	forty-first		s	41st	XLI

	Cardinal		Ordinal			Roman
50	fift*y*	*ies*	fiftieth	*s*	50th	L
51	fifty-one	*s*	fifty-first	*s*	51st	LI
60	sixt*y*	*ies*	sixtieth	*s*	60th	LX
61	sixty-one	*s*	sixty-first	*s*	61st	LXI
70	sevent*y*	*ies*	seventieth	*s*	70th	LXX
71	seventy-one	*s*	seventy-first	*s*	71st	LXXI
80	eight*y*	*ies*	eightieth	*s*	80th	LXXX
81	eighty-one	*s*	eighty-first	*s*	81st	LXXXI
90	ninet*y*	*ies*	nintieth	*s*	90th	XC
91	ninety-one	*s*	ninety-first	*s*	91st	XCI
100	hundred	*s*	hundredth	*s*	100th	C
500	five hundred		five hundreth		500th	D
1,000	thousand	*s*	thousandth	*s*	1,000th	M
10,000	ten thousand		ten thousandth		10,000th	
100,000	one hundred thousand		one hundred thousandth		100,000th	
1,000,000	million	*s*	millionth	*s*	1,000,000th	

Roman numerals

When a smaller number comes *before* a larger one, it is subtracted,
e.g. IV = 5 − 1 = 4; IX = 10 − 1 = 9; XL = 50 − 10 = 40; CD = 500 − 100 = 400

When a smaller number comes *after* a larger one, it is added,
e.g. VI = 5 + 1 = 6; XI = 10 + 1 = 11; LX = 50 + 10 = 60; DC = 500 + 100 = 600

Countries and Peoples of the World

Afghanistan	Afghan	s	Germany	German	s
Africa	African	s	Ghana	Ghanaian	s
Albania	Albanian	s	Greece	Greek	s
Algeria	Algerian	s	Greenland	Greenlander	s
America	American	s			
Angola	Angolan	s	Holland	Dutch	
Argentina	Argentinian	s	Hong Kong	—	
Asia	Asian	s	Hungary	Hungarian	s
Australia	Australian	s			
Austria	Austrian	s	Iceland	Icelander	s
			India	Indian	s
Bangladesh	Bengali	s	Indonesia	Indonesian	s
Barbados	Barbadian	s	Iran	Iranian	s
Belgium	Belgian	s	Iraq	Iraqi	s
Brazil	Brazilian	s	Ireland	Irish	
Britain	British, Briton	s	Israel	Israeli	s
Bulgaria	Bulgarian	s	Italy	Italian	s
Burma	Burmese				
			Jamaica	Jamaican	s
Cambodia	Cambodian	s	Japan	Japanese	
Canada	Canadian	s	Java	Javanese	
Chile	Chilean	s	Jordan	Jordanian	s
China	Chinese				
Cuba	Cuban	s	Kenya	Kenyan	s
Cyprus	Cypriot	s	Korea	Korean	s
Czechoslovakia	Czech	s			
			Lapland	Lapp	s
Denmark	Dane	s	Lebanon	Lebanese	
			Liberia	Liberian	s
Egypt	Egyptian	s	Libya	Libyan	s
Eire	Irish				
England	English		Malaya	Malayan	s
Ethiopia	Ethiopian	s	Malaysia	Malaysian	s
Europe	European	s	Malta	Maltese	
			Mexico	Mexican	s
Finland	Finn	s	Morocco	Moroccan	s
France	French		Mozambique	Mozambiquean	s

Namibia	Namibian	*s*	Tanzania	Tanzanian	*s*
Netherlands	Dutch		Thailand	Thai	*s*
New Zealand	New Zealander	*s*	Tibet	Tibetan	*s*
Nigeria	Nigerian	*s*	Trinidad	Trinidadian	*s*
Norway	Norwegian	*s*	Turkey	Turk	*s*
Pakistan	Pakistani	*s*	Uganda	Ugandan	*s*
Palestine	Palestinian	*s*	United States		
Peru	Peruvian	*s*	of America	American	*s*
Poland	Pole	*s*	Union of Soviet		
Portugal	Portuguese		Socialist	Soviet,	
			Republics	Russian	*s*
R(o)umania	R(o)umanian	*s*			
Russia	Russian	*s*	Venezuela	Venezuelan	*s*
			Vietnam	Vietnamese	
Saudi Arabia	Saudi (Arabian)	*s*			
Scandinavia	Scandinavian	*s*	Wales	Welsh	
Scotland	Scot	*s*	West Indies	West Indian	*s*
Singapore	Singaporean	*s*			
South Africa	South African	*s*	Yugoslavia	Yugoslav	*s*
Spain	Spanish,				
	Spaniard	*s*	Zaire	Zairean	*s*
Sri Lanka	Sin(g)halese		Zambia	Zambian	*o*
Sweden	Swede	*s*	Zimbabwe	Zimbabwean	*s*
Switzerland	Swiss				
Syria	Syrian	*s*			

Parts of Speech

Noun: A naming word, e.g. *boy, man, cat, house, Susan, England*.
On *Monday John* went by *coach* to *London Zoo* with his
teacher, *Mr. Smith*, and other *children* from his *class*.

Pronoun: A word used instead of a noun, e.g. *me, she, it, we, us, him*.
You and *I* will go now and *he* can come later with *them*.

Adjective: A word that is 'added to' a noun to describe it, e.g.
fat, thin, big, brown, green, ugly, pretty, delicious.
A *funny, little, old* man with a *large* nose and a *grey*
beard showed the *small* children his *beautiful* garden.

Verb: A doing word; a word that tells what is done, e.g.
do, go, stay, talk, shout, jump, lift, fight, eat, drink.
Stop running or you will *fall* and *hurt* yourself.

Adverb: A word that tells how, when or where something happens, e.g.
soon, often, there, now, never, quickly, carefully, carelessly.
Yesterday when I came *here* I jumped *over* that wall.

Preposition: A word that is placed before a noun, e.g.
by, in, into, at, for, under, over, against, near.
Bob went *with* his sister *on* a bus *to* the town.

Conjunction: A word that joins sentences, phrases or words, e.g.
or, than, though, although, because, while, unless.
John *and* Mary will go *if* it is fine *but* not *if* it rains.

Interjection: A word used as an exclamation, e.g. *Ah! Alas! Hey!*
Oh! You did frighten me. *Ouch!* That hurt.

Article: One of the three words – *a, an* or *the*.
A boy rode on *an* elephant at *the* zoo.

Spelling Lists of Words to Learn

The following lists contain the words you will need to use most often in your writing and compositions. You should, therefore, learn and try to remember how to spell all these words. Choose the shortest and easiest words at the beginning of each section to learn first. It is better to learn a few words each day rather than a long list, at one time, once a week. To make it easier for you the words are usually arranged in lists according to the number of letters in the words: three, four, five letters, etc. The number at the top of a word list shows the number of letters in each word in that list. Before you start to learn a list of words first study all the words in the list and notice that some words have the same letters in exactly the same order as others in the list.

All the words on pages 118 to 123 and at the bottom of page 126 are verbs, or may be used as verbs, and are arranged in lists according to the way in which their *ed, ing, s* endings are formed. When your teacher tests you on the words you have learnt he/she will probably ask you how to spell some of these words with their *ed, ing, s* endings to see whether you have understood this, e.g.

bark	**scare**	**drop**
mark *ed*	**score** *d*	**chop** *ped*
park *ing*	**stor** *ing*	**shop** *ping*
work *s*	**stone** *s*	**stop** *s*

You may add *ed, ing, s* to all the following words, e.g.

camp *ed, ing, s* = **camped, camping, camps**

3		4		4		4	
act	*ed, ing, s*	**book**	*ed, ing, s*	**back**	*ed, ing, s*	**camp**	*ed, ing, s*
add		**cook**		**pack**		**damp**	
air		**hook**		**sack**		**bump**	
arm		**look**		**dock**		**dump**	
ask		**cool**		**lock**		**jump**	
end		**pool**		**rock**		**lump**	
ink		**show**		**kick**		**pump**	
oil		**slow**		**lick**		**bomb**	
own		**flow**		**pick**		**comb**	
toy		**snow**		**tick**		**lamb**	

4		4		4		4	
dust	*ed, ing, s*	**call**	*ed, ing, s*	**bark**	*ed, ing, s*	**load**	*ed, ing, s*
last		**fell**		**mark**		**boat**	
list		**well**		**park**		**coat**	
nest		**yell**		**work**		**roar**	
rest		**fill**		**cork**		**soap**	
test		**kill**		**fork**		**help**	
post		**mill**		**milk**		**long**	
lift		**will**		**talk**		**hunt**	
melt		**pull**		**walk**		**want**	
salt		**roll**		**bank**		**word**	

4		4		4		4	
form	*ed, ing, s*	**gain**	*ed, ing, s*	**head**	*ed, ing, s*	**bath**	*ed, ing, s*
farm		**pain**		**heal**		**down**	
harm		**rain**		**heat**		**even**	
warm		**pair**		**seat**		**open**	
band		**fail**		**fear**		**turn**	
hand		**jail**		**near**		**join**	
land		**nail**		**team**		**iron**	
sand		**sail**		**play**		**part**	
bang		**tail**		**pray**		**mind**	
gang		**wait**		**stay**		**view**	

5			5			5			6		
clean	*ed, ing, s*		knock	*ed, ing, s*		thank	*ed, ing, s*		answer	*ed, ing, s*	
clear			clock			train			corner		
climb			block			tramp			flower		
cloud			shock			treat			bother		
clown			black			light			gather		
chain			crack			right			matter		
chair			track			sight			master		
chalk			brick			dream			murder		
cheer			trick			radio			number		
cheat			wreck			visit			wonder		

5			5			6			6		
enter	*ed, ing, s*		count	*ed, ing, s*		appear	*ed, ing, s*		remind	*ed, ing, s*	
cover			cough			arrest			return		
lower			rough			attack			reward		
offer			round			happen			school		
order			pound			hollow			scream		
water			sound			follow			stream		
paper			mouth			borrow			belong		
paint			group			button			poison		
point			scout			butter			powder		
plant			shout			letter			obtain		

5			5			6			7		
laugh	*ed, ing, s*		boast	*ed, ing, s*		colour	*ed, ing, s*		explain	*ed, ing, s*	
haunt			coast			doctor			contain		
field			roast			ground			curtain		
float			toast			garden			captain		
floor			start			awaken			holiday		
flood			stamp			fasten			journey		
bloom			storm			listen			present		
stoop			allow			pocket			pretend		
spoon			enjoy			rocket			soldier		
sport			guard			ticket			station		

5			6+			6+			7+		
crawl	*ed, ing, s*		expect	*ed, ing, s*		repair	*ed, ing, s*		disobey	*ed, ing, s*	
creak			collect			remain			discover		
crowd			correct			remind			disappear		
crown			protect			remember			disappoint		

You may add *ing* and *s* to the following words. You may not add *ed*. The words on the right of the columns are used instead.

buy	*ing, s* : **bought**	wear	*ing, s* : **wore, worn**
lay	: **laid**	ring	: **rang, rung**
pay	: **paid**	sing	: **sang, sung**
say	: **said**	spring	: **sprang, sprung**
cost	: **cost**	sink	: **sank, sunk**
feed	: **fed**	drink	: **drank, drunk**
feel	: **felt**	think	: **thought**
find	: **found**	bring	: **brought**
hear	: **heard**	fight	: **fought**
hold	: **held**	build	: **built**
hurt	*ing, s* : **hurt**	shoot	*ing, s* : **shot**
keep	: **kept**	sleep	: **slept**
lead	: **led**	stand	: **stood**
lend	: **lent**	spend	: **spent**
send	: **sent**	sweep	: **swept**
sell	: **sold**	swing	: **swung**
tell	: **told**	spread	: **spread**
meet	: **met**	break	: **broke,** *n*
mean	: **meant**	speak	: **spoke,** *n*
read	: **read**	steal	: **stole,** *n*
see	*n, ing, s* : **saw**	eat	*en, ing, s* : **ate**
blow	*n, ing, s* : **blew**	beat	*en, ing, s* : **beat**
draw	*n, ing, s* : **drew**	fall	*en, ing, s* : **fell**
grow	*n, ing, s* : **grew**		
know	*n, ing, s* : **knew**	catch	*ing, es* : **caught**
throw	*n, ing, s* : **threw**	teach	*ing, es* : **taught**

You may add *ed, ing, es* to all the following words:

box *ed, ing, es*	fish *ed, ing, es*	kiss *ed, ing, es*	fetch *ed, ing, es*
fix	dish	miss	match
mix	push	cross	watch
	rush	pass	scratch
	wash	class	march
	wish	grass	reach
	brush	guess	bunch
	crash	press	lunch
	flash	dress	touch
	finish	address	search

All the following words end in a consonant followed by a letter **e**.
You may add *d* and *s* to all the words but the **e** must be dropped before adding *ing*, e.g.

      hope   *d, øing, s* = **hoped, hoping, hopes**

4		4		4		5	
care *d, øing, s*		dive *d, øing, s*		hope *d, øing, s*		argue *d, øing, s*	
dare		tire		rope		blame	
face		fire		note		flame	
race		wire		hole		place	
save		wipe		love		dance	
wave		fine		move		piece	
hate		line		name		force	
bake		live		side		voice	
rake		like		time		price	
wake		hike		type		prize	

ø Drop **e** before adding *ing*

continued on page 122

5		5		6		6	
chase	*d, ȩing, s*	**scare**	*d, ȩing, s*	**battle**	*d, ȩing, s*	**arrive**	*d, ȩing, s*
close		**score**		**bottle**		**behave**	
cause		**store**		**settle**		**chance**	
pause		**stone**		**bubble**		**bridge**	
house		**smile**		**paddle**		**change**	
amuse		**serve**		**puzzle**		**charge**	
raise		**taste**		**bundle**		**garage**	
nurse		**waste**		**double**		**damage**	
sense		**brave**		**hurdle**		**manage**	
tease		**prove**		**single**		**voyage**	

6		7		7		8	
decide	*d, ȩing, s*	**balance**	*d, ȩing, s*	**picture**	*d, ȩing, s*	**surprise**	*d, ȩing, s*
divide		**bandage**		**promise**		**exercise**	
invite		**believe**		**provide**		**exchange**	
escape		**bicycle**		**prepare**		**celebrate**	
notice		**breathe**		**produce**		**continue**	
excuse		**deserve**		**grumble**		**decorate**	
refuse		**capture**		**stumble**		**describe**	
rescue		**explore**		**tremble**		**puncture**	
circle		**imagine**		**trouble**		**struggle**	
centre		**receive**		**whistle**		**treasure**	

All the words in the left-hand columns end in a consonant followed by a letter **e**. You may add *s* to all the words but the **e** must be dropped before adding *ing*.

You may not add *d*. The words on the right of the column are used instead.

come	*ȩing, s* : came	bite	*ȩing, s* : bit, bitten
make	: made	hide	: hid, hidden
lose	: lost	ride	: rode, ridden
leave	: left	rise	: rose, risen
slide	: slid	drive	: drove, driven
strike	: struck	write	: wrote, written
		choose	: chose, n

give	*n, ȩing, s* : gave
take	*n, ȩing, s* : took
shake	*n, ȩing, s* : shook
mistake	*n, ȩing, s* : mistook

ȩ Drop **e** before adding *ing*

You may add *s* to all the following words. The final consonant (the last letter) must be doubled before adding *ed, ing,*

e.g. **drop**   *ped, ping, s* = **dropped, dropping, drops**

3		3		3		4	
bat	*ted, ting, s*	**dip**	*ped, ping, s*	**beg**	*ged, ging, s*	**drop**	*ped, ping, s*
pat		**rip**		**peg**		**chop**	
pet		**tip**		**gag**		**shop**	
net		**zip**		**wag**		**stop**	
wet		**hop**		**hug**		**swop**	
fit		**pop**		**tug**		**ship**	
rot		**top**		**gun**		**slip**	
rob		**tap**		**sun**		**skip**	
mob		**map**		**pin**		**drip**	
sob		**yap**		**jab**		**grip**	

4		4		5+		5+	
trip	*ped, ping, s*	**plan**	*ned, ning, s*	**equal**	*led, ling, s*	**admit**	*ted, ting, s*
whip		**stun**		**signal**		**permit**	
clap		**grin**		**pencil**		**commit**	
snap		**skin**		**model**		**regret**	
trap		**skid**		**cancel**		**occur**	
wrap		**chat**		**parcel**		**refer**	
step		**plot**		**shovel**		**prefer**	
stab		**knot**		**travel**		**equip**	
grab		**knit**		**tunnel**		**kidnap**	
drag		**dial**		**quarrel**		**unwrap**	

None of the following words may end in *ed.*
The words in the right hand column are used instead.

get	*ting, s* : **got**		**dig**	*ging, s* : **dug**	
set	*ting, s* : **set**		**run**	*ning, s* : **ran**	
sit	*ting, s* : **sat**		**win**	*ning, s* : **won**	
hit	*ting, s* : **hit**		**spin**	*ning, s* : **spun**	
cut	*ting, s* : **cut**		**begin**	*ning, s* : **began, begun**	
shut	*ting, s* : **shut**		**swim**	*ming, s* : **swam, swum**	

You may add *er, est, ly, ness* to all the following words, e.g.

bold *er, est, ly, ness* = **bolder, boldest, boldly, boldness**

4		4+		5	
bold	*er, est, ly, ness*	**fair**	*er, est, ly, ness*	**light**	*er, est, ly, ness*
cold		**dear**		**tight**	
poor		**near**		**quick**	
cool		**neat**		**quiet**	
deep		**mean**		**queer**	
dark		**weak**		**steep**	
kind		**clean**		**sharp**	
loud		**clear**		**short**	
rich		**cheap**		**smart**	
slow		**great**		**thick**	
soft		**fresh**		**rough**	
wild		**clever**		**tough**	

You may add *r, st, ly, ness* to the following words:

4		4+	
late	*r, st, ly, ness*	**rude**	*r, st, ly, ness*
nice		**wide**	
fine		**large**	
safe		**close**	
sore		**fierce**	
sure		**strange**	

You may add *ly, ness* to the following words but
the last letter must be doubled before adding *er, est.*

3		3+	
sad	*der, dest, ly, ness*	**fat**	*ter, test*
mad	*der, dest*	**flat**	*ter, test*
hot	*ter, test*	**thin**	*ner, nest*
fit	*ter, test*		

All the following words end in y.
The y must be dropped before adding *ier, iest, ily, iness,*
e.g. **eas** y   *ier, iest, ily, iness* = **easier, easiest, easily, easiness**

4+

eas y   *ier, iest, ily, iness*
laz y
tid y
tin y
ugl y
dirt y
empt y
heav y
juic y
luck y
nois y
rock y

5

happ y *ier, iest, ily, iness*
sunn y
funn y
fuss y
mess y
mudd y
joll y
sill y
sorr y
shak y
wear y
wind y

6

stick y *ier, iest, ily, iness*
trick y
shabb y
prett y
lovel y
lonel y
sleep y
greed y
cheek y
breez y
gloom y
storm y

6+

hungr y *ier, iest, ily, iness*
cloud y
clums y
chill y
kindl y
stead y
untid y
unluck y
naught y
thirst y
health y
wealth y

4+

bus y   *ier, iest, ily*
angr y   *ier, iest, ily*
earl y   *ier, iest, iness*
sand y   *ier, iest, iness*
merr y   *ier, iest, ily, iment*

dough	also	Monday	January
cough	always	Tuesday	February
rough	almost	Wednesday	March
tough	although	Thursday	April
enough	already	Friday	May
plough	altogether	Saturday	June
through		Sunday	July
ought	all right		August
bought		spring	September
brought		summer	October
fought		autumn	November
thought		winter	December

All the following words end in **y**.
You may add *ing* but the **y** must be dropped before adding *ied, ies*.

cry	*ing*	**carry**	*ing*	**copy**	*ing*
cr*ied*	*ies*	**carr***ied*	*ies*	**cop***ied*	*ies*
dry	*ing*	**marry**	*ing*	**bury**	*ing*
dr*ied*	*ies*	**marr***ied*	*ies*	**bur***ied*	*ies*
try	*ing*	**hurry**	*ing*	**tidy**	*ing*
tr*ied*	*ies*	**hurr***ied*	*ies*	**tid***ied*	*ies*
fry	*ing*	**worry**	*ing*	**occupy**	*ing*
fr*ied*	*ies*	**worr***ied*	*ies*	**occup***ied*	*ies*
spy	*ing*	**empty**	*ing*	**satisfy**	*ing*
sp*ied*	*ies*	**empt***ied*	*ies*	**satisf***ied*	*ies*
fly	*ing*	**study**	*ing*	**terrify**	*ing*
fl*ies*		**stud***ied*	*ies*	**terrif***ied*	*ies*
flew, flown					

A very few verbs end in **ie**. You may add *d* and *s* but the **ie** must be changed to *y* before adding *ing*.

die	*d, s*	**lie**	*d, s*	**tie**	*d, s*
dy*ing*		**ly***ing*		**ty***ing*	

Singular	Plural	Singular	Plural	Singular	Plural
foot	feet	bab*y*	*ies*	key	*s*
goose	geese	lad*y*	*ies*	donkey	*s*
tooth	teeth	bod*y*	*ies*	monkey	*s*
mouse	mice	pon*y*	*ies*	valley	*s*
man	men	cit*y*	*ies*	chimney	*s*
woman	women	arm*y*	*ies*	cowboy	*s*
child	children	nav*y*	*ies*	railway	*s*
		aunt*y*	*ies*	gangway	*s*
life	lives	dadd*y*	*ies*	holiday	*s*
wife	wives	mumm*y*	*ies*	birthday	*s*
knife	knives				
		dais*y*	*ies*	zoo	*s*
leaf	leaves	dair*y*	*ies*	piano	*s*
loaf	loaves	fair*y*	*ies*	radio	*s*
thief	thieves	stor*y*	*ies*		
		part*y*	*ies*	hero	*es*
dwarf *s or*	dwarves	jell*y*	*ies*	cargo	*es*
scarf *s or*	scarves	lorr*y*	*ies*	Negro	*es*
wharf *s or*	wharves	pupp*y*	*ies*	potato	*es*
hoof *s or*	hooves	hobb*y*	*ies*	tomato	*es*
roof *s*		enem*y*	*ies*	volcano	*es*
elf	elves	canar*y*	*ies*	bus	*es*
calf	calves	famil*y*	*ies*	glass	*es*
half	halves	grann*y*	*ies*	beach	*es*
wolf	wolves	cherr*y*	*ies*	peach	*es*
shelf	shelves	countr*y*	*ies*	torch	*es*
		librar*y*	*ies*	witch	*es*
self	selves	factor*y*	*ies*	church	*es*
itself		robber*y*	*ies*	circus	*es*
myself		myster*y*	*ies*	princess	*es*
himself		discover*y*	*ies*	sandwich	*es*
herself					
yourself	yourselves	**every**	*body, one, thing, where*		
	ourselves	**any**	*body, one, thing, where, how, way*		
	themselves	**some**	*body, one, thing, where, how, times*		

4	4	5	4		4		5	
able	than	these	bell	s	bird	s	giant	s
away	that	those	ball	s	desk	s	glove	s
best	then	where	wall	s	lake	s	green	s
born	them	which	hall	s	lawn	s	hedge	s
both	they	while	hill	s	lion	s	horse	s
does	this	whole	cake	s	neck	s	hotel	s
done	true	whose	card	s	nose	s	jewel	s
goes	luck	worse	cart	s	page	s	lemon	s
gone	ever	worst	cave	s	path	s	noise	s
gold	very	worth	case	s	pond	s	ocean	s

4	4	5	4		4		5	
dead	went	could	coal	s	shed	s	other	s
deaf	were	would	goal	s	shoe	s	owner	s
each	what	magic	door	s	sock	s	plate	s
else	when	might	food	s	song	s	fruit	s
just	with	money	moon	s	tent	s	pupil	s
must	clay	music	room	s	town	s	purse	s
much	beef	never	wood	s	tree	s	queen	s
many	pork	pence	wool	s	mile	s	salad	s
more	east	sugar	flag	s	your	s	shirt	s
most	west	ready	frog	s	year	s	snake	s

4	5	5	4		5		5	
from	about	among	game	s	apple	s	stair	s
next	above	below	gate	s	baker	s	stick	s
none	after	blood	gift	s	bread	s	stove	s
only	again	earth	hole	s	beast	s	sword	s
once	ahead	often	home	s	cabin	s	table	s
upon	alone	sorry	hour	s	cloth	s	thing	s
same	along	sheep	king	s	comic	s	tiger	s
some	alike	shall	kite	s	dozen	s	truck	s
soon	alive	under	knee	s	front	s	white	s
such	aside	until	idea	s	ghost	s	world	s

6	7	6		6		9	
across	against	friend	s	infant	s	adventure	s
afraid	another	forest	s	insect	s	aeroplane	s
around	because	finger	s	inside	s	afternoon	s
asleep	beneath	father	s	island	s	chocolate	s
ashore	between	mother	s	desert	s	favourite	s
awhile	clothes	leader	s	orange	s	passenger	s
before	instead	reader	s	second	s	newspaper	s
behind	nothing	saucer	s	minute	s	orchestra	s
better	perhaps	sister	s	moment	s	programme	s
cattle	without	reason	s	museum	s	vegetable	s

6	8	6		7		full	y
during	together	bullet	s	bedroom	s	awful	ly
either	tomorrow	carrot	s	blanket	s	useful	ly
famous	horrible	coffee	s	brother	s	careful	ly
hardly	horribly	cotton	s	teacher	s	playful	ly
little	terrible	dinner	s	sausage	s	cheerful	ly
middle	terribly	kitten	s	cabbage	s	dreadful	ly
modern	possible	lesson	s	cottage	s	thankful	ly
unless	possibly	rabbit	s	message	s	beautiful	ly
utmost	probable	robber	s	village	s	forgetful	ly
within	probably	rubber	s	lettuce	s	wonderful	ly

6	6		6		7			
people	animal	s	parent	s	chicken	s	helpful	ly
petrol	banana	s	person	s	kitchen	s	hopeful	ly
plenty	beside	s	prince	s	husband	s	skilful	ly
police	bucket	s	secret	s	pudding	s	faithful	ly
rather	castle	s	street	s	morning	s	grateful	ly
really	cousin	s	string	s	evening	s	peaceful	ly
safety	coward	s	violin	s	tadpole	s	powerful	ly
should	danger	s	window	s	tractor	s	spiteful	ly
seldom	engine	s	pillow	s	visitor	s	delightful	ly
silver	needle	s	yellow	s	outside	s	disgraceful	ly

Contractions *(shortened words)*

These are words which have been shortened by joining two words
together and placing an apostrophe where a letter or letters have been left out.
Learn the words and the contractions, being very careful to remember
exactly where the apostrophe goes.

can't = cannot
don't = do not
won't = will not
isn't = is not
aren't = are not
didn't = did not
hadn't = had not
hasn't = has not
wasn't = was not
shan't = shall not
doesn't = does not
haven't = have not
mustn't = must not
needn't = need not
weren't = were not
couldn't = could not
wouldn't = would not
shouldn't = should not

he's = he is;   he has
she's = she is;   she has
it's = it is
who's = who is
that's = that is
what's = what is
here's = here is
there's = there is

I'll = I will;   I shall
we'll = we will;   we shall
he'll = he will;   he shall
she'll = she will;   she shall
you'll = you will;   you shall
who'll = who will;   who shall
they'll = they will;   they shall

I'd = I had;   I would
he'd = he had;   he would
we'd = we had;   we would
you'd = you had;   you would
who'd = who had;   who would
they'd = they had;   they would

we're = we are
you're = you are
who're = who are
they're = they are

I've = I have
we've = we have
you've = you have
they've = they have

I'm = I am

The apostrophe is also used to show possession, e.g.

The boy's book;   girl's coat;   man's car;   woman's watch.
The boys' books;   girls' coats;   men's cars;   women's watches.

Homophones

These are words that sound alike but have different meanings and spellings.

arc	(curve)	**pain**	(suffering)	**accept**	(receive)
ark	(boat; box)	**pane**	(of glass)	**except**	(leaving out)
beach	(seashore)	**pair**	(two)	**allowed**	(let; permitted)
beech	(tree)	**pear**	(fruit)	**aloud**	(loudly)
bean	(plant)	**peace**	(quiet)	**altar**	(church table)
been	(past of be)	**piece**	(a part)	**alter**	(change)
blew	(blow)	**peer**	(stare)	**dear**	(beloved; costly)
blue	(colour)	**pier**	(jetty)	**deer**	(animal)
bough	(branch)	**place**	(position)	**flour**	(ground wheat)
bow	(bend)	**plaice**	(fish)	**flower**	(blossom)
brake	(to stop)	**rap**	(knock)	**foul**	(dirty; unfair)
break	(to snap)	**wrap**	(cover)	**fowl**	(bird)
chute	(a slide)	**sail**	(ship)	**freeze**	(ice; cold)
shoot	(fire)	**sale**	(selling)	**frieze**	(wall decoration)
die	(lose life)	**slay**	(kill)	**groan**	(moan)
dye	(colour)	**sleigh**	(sled)	**grown**	(got bigger)
farther	(further)	**stair**	(step)	**guessed**	(did guess)
father	(parent)	**stare**	(look at)	**guest**	(visitor)
fort	(castle)	**steal**	(thieve)	**hear**	(listen)
fought	(fight)	**steel**	(metal)	**here**	(in this place)
hair	(of head)	**tail**	(end)	**heard**	(listened)
hare	(animal)	**tale**	(story)	**herd**	(of cattle, etc.)
hart	(stag)	**pail**	(bucket)	**hoard**	(hidden store)
heart	(of body)	**pale**	(whitish)	**horde**	(crowd)
heal	(cure)	**scene**	(view; place)	**hour**	(sixty minutes)
heel	(of foot)	**seen**	(noticed)	**our**	(belonging to us)
higher	(taller)	**tire**	(weary)	**hole**	(hollow place)
hire	(rent)	**tyre**	(wheel cover)	**whole**	(all; complete)
hoarse	(husky)	**weak**	(not strong)	**meat**	(flesh)
horse	(animal)	**week**	(seven days)	**meet**	(come together)
leant	(leaned)	**weather**	(climate)	**meter**	(measuring box)
lent	(lend)	**whether**	(if)	**metre**	(length measure)
made	(make)	**wood**	(timber)	**moan**	(groan)
maid	(girl)	**would**	(past of will)	**mown**	(cut grass, etc.)
muscle	(of body)	**won**	(did win)	**signet**	(seal, ring)
mussel	(shellfish)	**one**	(single)	**cygnet**	(young swan)

knew	(know)	**shore**	(seashore)
new	(just made)	**sure**	(certain)
knight	(Sir)	**their**	(belonging to them)
night	(opp. of day)	**there**	(in that place)
know	(understand)	**they're**	(they are)
no	(not any; opp. of yes)	**theirs**	(belonging to them)
knot	(tied string, etc.)	**there's**	(there is)
not	(no)	**threw**	(throw)
passed	(did pass)	**through**	(from end to end)
past	(time gone by)	**throne**	(king's seat)
ring	(circle; bell sound)	**thrown**	(throw)
wring	(twist)	**board**	(wood; go on ship; lodge)
wait	(stay; serve)	**bored**	(weary; drilled hole)
weight	(Heaviness)	**cereal**	(wheat, oats, etc.)
way	(direction)	**serial**	(in parts)
weigh	(measure heaviness)	**currant**	(fruit)
waste	(not used; useless)	**current**	(flow of water, air, etc.)
waist	(of body)	**cue**	(hint; billiard-stick)
which	(what one? who?)	**queue**	(line of persons, etc.)
witch	(old woman)	**fair**	(just; light; entertainment)
who's	(who is)	**fare**	(price of journey; food)
whose	(belonging to whom?)	**core**	(middle of apple, etc.)
you're	(you are)	**corps**	(group of cadets, etc.)
your	(belonging to you)	**road**	(highway)
it's	(it is)	**rode**	(ride)
its	(belonging to it)	**rowed**	(used oars)
pedal	(foot lever)	**cent**	(coin)
peddle	(to hawk goods)	**sent**	(send)
hall	(room; passage)	**scent**	(smell; perfume)
haul	(pull; amount taken)	**rain**	(water)
him	(he)	**reign**	(rule)
hymn	(song of praise)	**rein**	(strap)
mare	(female horse)	**buy**	(purchase)
mayor	(head of town or city)	**by**	(near to, etc.)
medal	(badge – for bravery, etc.)	**bye**	(a run)
meddle	(interfere)	**to**	(towards)
pray	(ask God)	**too**	(also; more than enough)
prey	(victim; thing hunted)	**two**	(number)

Multiplication Tables

0 × 2 = 0	0 × 3 = 0	0 × 4 = 0	0 × 5 = 0
1 × 2 = 2	1 × 3 = 3	1 × 4 = 4	1 × 5 = 5
2 × 2 = 4	2 × 3 = 6	2 × 4 = 8	2 × 5 = 10
3 × 2 = 6	3 × 3 = 9	3 × 4 = 12	3 × 5 = 15
4 × 2 = 8	4 × 3 = 12	4 × 4 = 16	4 × 5 = 20
5 × 2 = 10	5 × 3 = 15	5 × 4 = 20	5 × 5 = 25
6 × 2 = 12	6 × 3 = 18	6 × 4 = 24	6 × 5 = 30
7 × 2 = 14	7 × 3 = 21	7 × 4 = 28	7 × 5 = 35
8 × 2 = 16	8 × 3 = 24	8 × 4 = 32	8 × 5 = 40
9 × 2 = 18	9 × 3 = 27	9 × 4 = 36	9 × 5 = 45
10 × 2 = 20	10 × 3 = 30	10 × 4 = 40	10 × 5 = 50
11 × 2 = 22	11 × 3 = 33	11 × 4 = 44	11 × 5 = 55
12 × 2 = 24	12 × 3 = 36	12 × 4 = 48	12 × 5 = 60

0 × 6 = 0	0 × 7 = 0	0 × 8 = 0	0 × 9 = 0
1 × 6 = 6	1 × 7 = 7	1 × 8 = 8	1 × 9 = 9
2 × 6 = 12	2 × 7 = 14	2 × 8 = 16	2 × 9 = 18
3 × 6 = 18	3 × 7 = 21	3 × 8 = 24	3 × 9 = 27
4 × 6 = 24	4 × 7 = 28	4 × 8 = 32	4 × 9 = 36
5 × 6 = 30	5 × 7 = 35	5 × 8 = 40	5 × 9 = 45
6 × 6 = 36	6 × 7 = 42	6 × 8 = 48	6 × 9 = 54
7 × 6 = 42	7 × 7 = 49	7 × 8 = 56	7 × 9 = 63
8 × 6 = 48	8 × 7 = 56	8 × 8 = 64	8 × 9 = 72
9 × 6 = 54	9 × 7 = 63	9 × 8 = 72	9 × 9 = 81
10 × 6 = 60	10 × 7 = 70	10 × 8 = 80	10 × 9 = 90
11 × 6 = 66	11 × 7 = 77	11 × 8 = 88	11 × 9 = 99
12 × 6 = 72	12 × 7 = 84	12 × 8 = 96	12 × 9 = 108

0 × 10 = 0	0 × 11 = 0	0 × 12 = 0
1 × 10 = 10	1 × 11 = 11	1 × 12 = 12
2 × 10 = 20	2 × 11 = 22	2 × 12 = 24
3 = 10 = 30	3 × 11 = 33	3 × 12 = 36
4 × 10 = 40	4 × 11 = 44	4 × 12 = 48
5 × 10 = 50	5 × 11 = 55	5 × 12 = 60
6 × 10 = 60	6 × 11 = 66	6 × 12 = 72
7 × 10 = 70	7 × 11 = 77	7 × 12 = 84
8 × 10 = 80	8 × 11 = 88	8 × 12 = 96
9 × 10 = 90	9 × 11 = 99	9 × 12 = 108
10 × 10 = 100	10 × 11 = 110	10 × 12 = 120
11 × 10 = 110	11 × 11 = 121	11 × 12 = 132
12 × 10 = 120	12 × 11 = 132	12 × 12 = 144

Note for Teachers and Parents

Spell It Yourself is based on the belief that there is need for a new type of book which is neither a dictionary nor a conventional spelling book.

Most school children are encouraged to refer to dictionaries for words they wish to use in their written work. But school dictionaries have been compiled, in the first place, for the giving of definitions: the choice of words is usually dictated by children's problems of understanding rather than of spelling. As a result, many everyday words which nevertheless present spelling difficulties are not in school dictionaries, because children are sure to know their meaning.

Some of the commonest spelling errors are made in forming derivatives from root-words which in themselves are quite easy to spell. For example, a child probably knows—or could easily find from a dictionary—how to spell these infinitives: differ, prefer, happen, begin, come, singe, sail, dial, shop, gallop, argue, agree, queue, picnic,,deny, tie, forget, fidget. But there will probably be nothing in the dictionary to help the child to the correct spelling of their present and past participles. How is he or she to know, for example, that the correct forms are 'shopping, shopped', and not 'shoping, shoped'? If the child remembers the doubling of that final consonant, how is he or she to know that the mistake of 'picnicing, picniced' must be corrected by writing 'picnicking, picnicked', and not 'picniccing, picnicced'? Other difficult and irregular word-derivatives not usually in dictionaries include plurals and the comparatives and superlatives of adjectives.

Certain spelling rules may be worked out, but most of these are confused by their many exceptions, and so are of limited usefulness, especially with younger children.

Clearly, children are likely to learn to spell correctly words which they are anxious to use in their own writing. In free writing, children are often not content to mis-spell, if they can avoid it; and they may waste much time, at the expense of the content of their written work, trying to discover the correct spelling of words they need. The usual school spelling-books of groups of words for memorization, children's own word-books, and most junior dictionaries cannot give proper guidance. The teacher often has little time to help with individual problems. It is hoped that this book, *Spell It Yourself*, will provide a useful tool, easy for children to handle for themselves as they need.

Spelling—with the exception of a limited number of the commonest words—seems a subject for individual learning: no two children wish to make use of exactly the same words in their written expression. This reference list, of nearly 8,000 root words, is based upon word-frequency in the upper classes of Junior and Middle Schools; but the list also includes many of the less common words which individual children may need.

In their written compositions children use words whose meanings they understand. They do not often need definitions of the words they cannot spell. Children's ability to read and recognize words is much greater than their ability to spell them; in this book they should be able quickly to find and identify the words they hesitate to spell. The order of the words is alphabetical, and if a child knows the first two letters—as he or she usually does—of the word required, the child can find in the Index the number of the page where he or she should look for it.

The alphabetical basis of the book provides useful training in the use of a dictionary. At the same time, *Spell It Yourself* makes a point of including many words which a school dictionary does not. Word-derivatives are usually shown by suffixes to the right of the columns which need only to be added to the root-words (see the Instructions).

In general, children learn best by finding out for themselves. In this book they will learn to look up words for themselves and to spell them correctly the first time, instead of making mistakes which have later to be corrected. They will steadily increase their written vocabulary, becoming more 'word-conscious' all the time. With this book at their elbow, and under the direction of a teacher aware of its purpose, they will be teaching themselves how to spell.

Index